Open Source Software

Making Business Applications accessible

Els **Van Vossel**

Fabien **Pinckaers**

# Drive your Sales & Marketing Activities with

## Close Leads, Automate Marketing Campaigns and Get Accurate Forecasts

Open Object Press

Open Source Software
Making Business Applications accessible to All Companies

Open ERP

# Drive your Sales & Marketing Activities with Open ERP:

## Best sales practices, build lasting relationships

by Els Van Vossel and Fabien Pinckaers




First Edition





Open Object Press

**Open Object Press** is a division of **OpenERP S.A.** (www.openerp.com)





First edition April 2011 **ISBN :** 978-2-9600876-1-1

Open Object Press

40, Chaussée de Namur
1367 Grand-Rosière
http://openerp.com/

*Special Thanks to Marc Laporte, Olivier Laurent, Gary Malherbe and Grégory Dethier*

Open Object Press

40, Chaussée de Namur
1367 Grand-Rosière
http://openerp.com/

*From the same Editor*

**OpenERP for Retail and Industrial Management – Steps towards Sales, Logistics and Manufacturing Integration, 2009, Fabien Pinckaers and Geoff Gardiner, ISBN: 978-2-9600876-0-4**

*The Authors: Els Van Vossel and Fabien Pinckaers*

# Contents

# Foreword

Information Systems have played an increasingly visible role over the past several years in improving the competitiveness of business. They are more than just tools for handling repetitive tasks; they will guide and advance all of a company's daily activities. Integrated Management Software is today very often a key source of significant competitive advantage.

## Open Source Software: Making Business Applications accessible

Some may look at the Business Application market as a mature market dominated by a few large key players, with no new business opportunities.

This would be ignoring the market reality. So many customers are frustrated by their experience with existing vendors; so many companies around the world need to have access to business applications, but cannot afford them.

OpenERP believes that business applications should not be a luxury. That any company, anywhere in the world, should be able to afford the best tools to professionally expand business. That is one of the reasons why OpenERP needs to break the existing rules of the ERPs and the Business Applications market.

Customers should use their budget smartly and invest in customizing the application to their specific needs, rather than paying expensive license fees. OpenERP is committed to the Open Source Business Model precisely because Open Source allows for this. Open Source is a disruptive model, as it creates more value for the customers.

For decades, customers have developed applications which remained specific to their own needs, and in the end proved extremely expensive to maintain. Open Source means that customers can benefit from past developments of other companies. Also by contributing to the evolution of the software, the users will enjoy the guarantee that their development will be included in future versions of the software. One of the major advantages is that such a *Community* brings a wealth of new functionality.

Open Source also allows us to engage with our customers differently. Since there is no licensing cost, any potential customer can download, test and use the software. OpenERP has no need for an expensive sales force to promote the product. OpenERP just needs to make the best product and make it available to customers.

Open Source allows for many barriers in this industry to be broken. The software is available to many companies who could otherwise not afford expensive business applications license fees. The OpenERP solution allows customers to use their money smartly and tailor the software to their individual needs. OpenERP leverages from its customer base to enrich the software and finally eradicate any lock-in to allow customers to use and even drop the software freely.

## The OpenERP Solution

OpenERP can build a new breed of business applications, more modular, more customer-friendly, fully web-based, which others cannot due to the heritage of their legacy systems.

OpenERP is a comprehensive suite of business applications including Sales, CRM, Project management, Warehouse management, Manufacturing, Financial management, and Human Resources, just to name a few. More than 1000 OpenERP modules are available from the OpenERP Apps market place (http://apps.openerp.com/).

The key to continued sales success is effective Customer Relationship Management, and that is precisely the main topic of the book you are reading. OpenERP's CRM and Sales features are flexible and highly developed to assist you in managing all aspects of partner relationships.

OpenERP can share information with the most common email clients, calendars and mobile phones, allowing your staff to build on previous productivity and experience by continuing to use familiar email and office systems, now connected to OpenERP. In a few clicks, your sales person can transfer necessary information to the OpenERP software. You can link important emails to the CRM directly from your current mailbox and even reply from your own mailbox and have the answer stored in your CRM automatically.

## Structure of this book

Part One, *First Steps with OpenERP* (page 1), starts with the basic steps to install OpenERP. You will also be introduced to the main concepts, such as Sales Teams & Stages, and you will be guided through a complete workflow, from Quotation to Sales Order. Part One also presents the OpenERP Online offer (SaaS solution), and the configuration wizards in the *Getting Started with OpenERP Online* (page 5) chapter. To discover OpenERP's features, you can jump directly to Part Two.

Part Two, *Managing Customer Acquisition* (page 21) explains you how to manage your customer relationships with OpenERP. You will learn more about how to manage Leads and Opportunities, to integrate existing communication tools with OpenERP, to efficiently manage a sales and channel department, and to monitor performance.

Part Three, *Driving your Marketing Campaigns* (page 77), is devoted to Direct Marketing. In a step-by-step tutorial, we will guide you through the process of setting up a marketing campaign in OpenERP.

Part Four, *Closing your Deals: from Quotation to Sales Order* (page 97), guides you from quotation to sales order, explaining several advanced sales features.

Finally part Five, *Installing & Configuring your OpenERP* (page 137), explains the detailed installation procedures for OpenERP. This chapter also explains how to install the Thunderbird & Outlook plugins, to get the most out of your existing email programs.

# About the authors

## Fabien Pinckaers

Fabien Pinckaers was only eighteen years old when he started his first company. Today, over ten years later, he has founded and managed several new technology companies, all based on Free / Open Source software.

He originated Tiny ERP, now OpenERP, and is the director of two companies including OpenERP S.A., the editor of OpenERP. In a few years time, he has grown the Tiny group from one to sixty-five employees without loans or external fund-raising, and while making a profit.

He has also developed several large scale projects, such as Auction-in-Europe.com, which became the leader in the art market in Belgium. Even today people sell more art works there than on ebay.be.

He is also the founder of the LUG (Linux User Group) of Louvain-la-Neuve, and of several free projects like OpenReport, OpenStuff and Tiny Report. Educated as a civil engineer (polytechnic), he has won several IT prizes in Europe such as Wired and l'Inscene.

A fierce defender of free software in the enterprise, he is in constant demand as a conference speaker and he is the author of numerous articles dealing with free software in the management of the enterprise.

Follow Fabien on his blog http://fptiny.blogspot.com/ or on twitter fpopenerp.

## Els Van Vossel

Els Van Vossel always had a dedication to both written and spoken word. Clear and explicit communication is crucial.

Educated as a Professional Translator in Antwerp, she worked as an independent translator on the localization of major ERP software. Els acquired ERP knowledge and decided to start working as a functional ERP consultant and a Technical Communicator for ERP software.

As such, the world of OpenSource software became more and more attractive. She started working with OpenERP software in her free time and doing so, Els really wanted to meet Fabien Pinckaers to share thoughts about documentation and training strategy. At a Partner Meeting she heard Fabien was looking for someone to manage the trainings & documentation. This was absolutely an opportunity to be qualified, and now Els is the OpenERP Training Program Manager and in this job responsible for the worldwide training and certification program of OpenERP.

Being an author of several Software Manuals, she finds it exciting to work on the OpenERP documentation and continuously take it to a higher level. Please note that this is a hell of a job, but Els finds great pleasure in doing it!

Follow Els on her blog http://training-openerp.blogspot.com/ or on twitter elsvanvossel.

# Acknowledgements

*From Els Van Vossel*

Thank you Fabien, for offering me the opportunity to work with OpenERP. I thank all OpenERP team members for their support and understanding. My special thanks to my family who encouraged me to write this book.

*From Fabien Pinckaers*

I address my thanks to all of the team at OpenERP for their hard work in preparing, translating and re-reading the book in its various forms. My particular thanks to Laurence Henrion and my family for supporting me throughout all this effort.

# Part I

# First Steps with OpenERP

OpenERP is an impressive software system, being easy to use and yet providing great benefits in helping you manage your company. It is easy to install under both Windows and Linux compared with other enterprise-scale systems, and offers unmatched functionality.

# Installation and Initial Setup 1

Whether you want to test OpenERP or put it into full production, you have at least two possible starting points:

- you can use OpenERP Online by subscribing to http://www.openerp.com/online/;
- you can install the solution on your own computers to test it in your company's system environment.

In this chapter, the easy-to-use *OpenERP Online* solution will be briefly explained. For more information about installing OpenERP on your computer, please refer to the chapter *Installing & Configuring your OpenERP* (page 137).

**Some Interesting Websites from OpenERP**

- Main Site: http://www.openerp.com,
- OpenERP Online Site: http://www.openerp.com/online,
- Online demo at http://demo.openerp.com,
- Documentation site: http://doc.openerp.com/,
- Community discussion forum where you can often receive assistance: http://www.openerp.com/forum/.

**Current documentation**

The procedure for installing OpenERP and its web server are likely to change and improve with each new version, so you should always check each release's documentation on the website for the latest installation procedures.

## 1.1 Use OpenERP Online

Nothing is easier for you to discover OpenERP than subscribing to the OpenERP Online offer. You just need a web browser to get started.

The Online service can be particularly useful to small companies, that just want to get going quickly at low cost. You have immediate access to OpenERP's Integrated Management System built on the type of enterprise architecture used in many organizations.

OpenERP's Online offer includes several services: hosting at high bandwidth, database management, stable security update, backups, maintenance (24/7 server monitoring), bug fixing and migrations.

OpenERP guarantees that the software running on OpenERP Online is exactly the same as the Open Source official version of OpenERP. Any improvement made on OpenERP will be available online. This allows you to easily switch from the online version to the local version anytime.

So even if the OpenERP Online solution might be the best solution to suit your needs today, you can easily switch to an installation on your own servers according to your company's changing requirements or growth. You are also able to change your service provider anytime, while continuing to use the exact same system. Hence, you do not depend on your host. In addition, OpenERP works with standard and open formats and programming languages which allow you to export your data and use them in any other software.

These advantages give you total control over your data, your software, your platform.

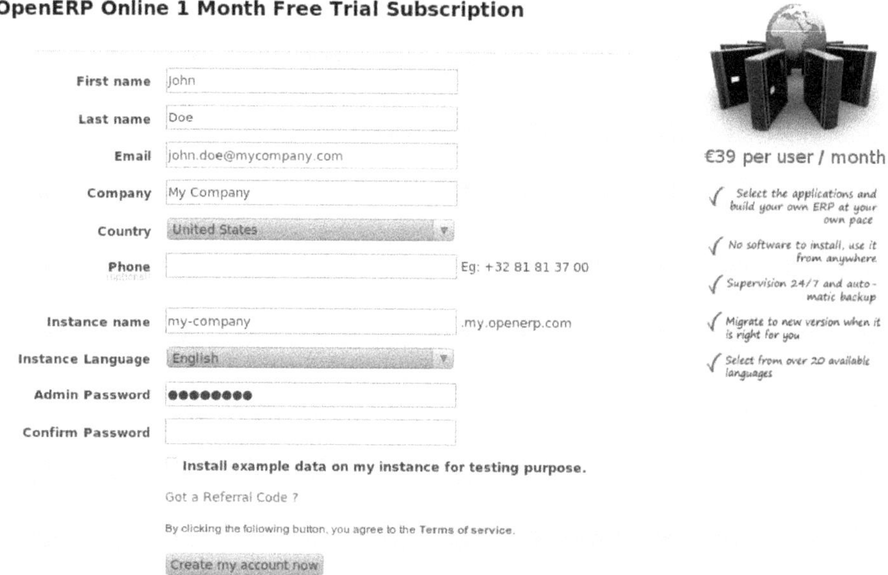


Figure 1.1: *Subscribe and Start with OpenERP Online*

If you want to start working with the online platform, you can navigate to http://www.openerp.com/online. After successful registration, you will be able to configure and use OpenERP online. To log in to your OpenERP Online account, you will receive a username and password. You can build the software to fit your needs, at your own pace!

OpenERP Online - Software as a Service - is hosted by OpenERP and paid in the form of a monthly subscription. The pricing model is extremely simple. OpenERP charges a fixed fee per month per user. You will get an invoice each month according to the number of users registered in the system at that time. If you add new users during the next 30 days, they will only be charged with the next invoice. You can find the details of current pricing and payment options at http://www.openerp.com/online.

**Free Trial**

For a month's free trial, check out OpenERP's http://www.openerp.com/online, which enables you to get started quickly without incurring costs for integration or for buying computer systems. After the free trial expires, you can easily continue using OpenERP Online.

## 1.2 Getting Started with OpenERP Online

If you want to focus on your customers, you need tools: to capture all the knowledge you have available; to help you analyze what you know; to make it easy to use all of that knowledge and analysis. OpenERP invites you to discover the CRM & Sales Management Business Application!

In this chapter, you can start exploring OpenERP!

Use a web browser of your choice to connect to OpenERP Web.

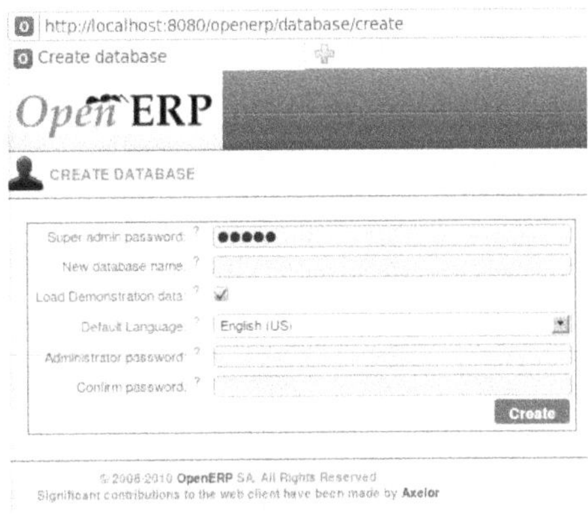


Figure 1.2: *Web Client at Startup*

OpenERP suggests that you configure your database using a series of questions. In the software, these series of questions are managed through so-called `Configuration Wizards`.

Click the `Start Configuration` button to continue.

The next configuration wizard will help you to decide what your user interface will look like, whether the screens will only show the most important fields - `Simplified` - or whether you also want to see the fields for the more advanced users, the `Extended` view. Select `Extended` and click *Next* to continue.

**User Preferences**

You can easily switch from Simplified to Extended view by changing your *User Preferences*.

In the next wizard, you can fill your company data, select your company's base currency and add your company logo which can be printed on reports. Click *Next* to continue.

Select the `Customer Relationship Management` and `Sales Management` business applications for installation and click *Install*. Now OpenERP will start to install CRM & Sales, allowing you to do a complete sales cycle, from lead / opportunity to quotation and sales order. You will have to wait for the next configuration wizard to be displayed (*Loading* will appear).

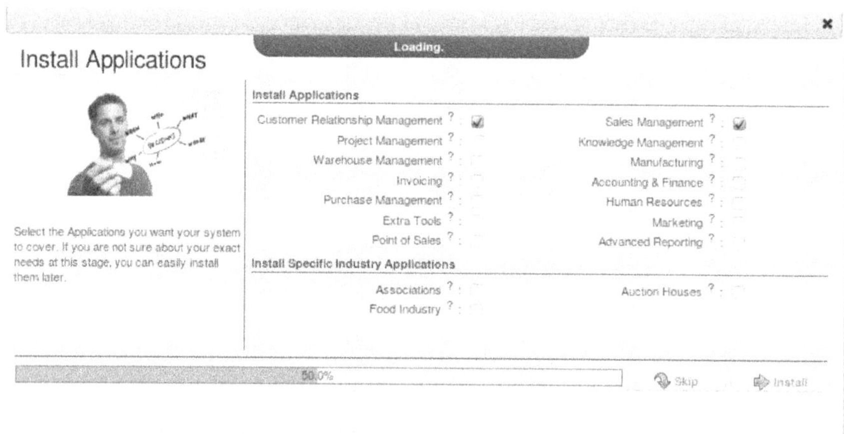


Figure 1.3: *Selecting the CRM & Sales Functionality*

OpenERP's modularity enables you to install a single Business Application (such as CRM) if that is all you need. Of course, you can choose to also install Sales Management, to handle quotations, sales orders and sales invoices as well. For now, please install `Customer Relationship Management` and `Sales Management`, as these two Business Applications will be discussed in this book.

**Reconfigure**

Keep in mind that you can change or reconfigure the system any time, for instance through the *Reconfigure* option in the main bar.

When you choose a business application for installation, OpenERP will automatically propose to add or configure related (smaller) applications to enrich your system. When you install CRM, OpenERP will also ask you whether you want to install Fetchmail, or Sales FAQ, for instance.

The figure *Selecting Accounting Configuration* (page 7) shows the Accounting Application Configuration screen that appears when you select `Sales Management` to be installed.

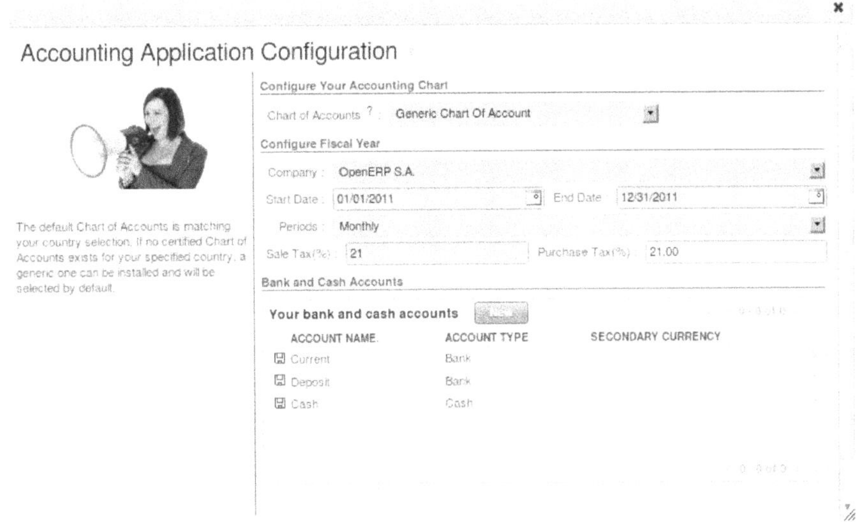


Figure 1.4: *Selecting Accounting Configuration*

Indeed, accounting is required to create sales invoices. Select the *Generic Chart of Account* and fill in the Sale Tax (%) applicable in your country. Click *Configure* to continue the configuration.

**Accounting**

Please note that you can perfectly well use OpenERP's CRM without doing your accounting in OpenERP. When you only install CRM, there is no need to configure accounting.

OpenERP CRM offers lots of features. You can easily manage your address book (prospects, customers, ...), keep track of leads and/or opportunities, manage meetings & phone calls, share (sales) knowledge and much more.

The figure *Selecting CRM Configuration* (page 8) shows the CRM Application Configuration screen that appears when you select `Customer Relationship Management` to be installed.

To stay in line with what will be described later in this book, please install the following options:

- `Opportunity to Quotation` will be checked by default, allowing you to create quotations from an opportunity,
- `Sale FAQ` to install a company wiki to share your sales knowledge,
- `Calendar Synchronizing` to link your OpenERP calendar to your mobile device, for instance,
- `Fetch Emails` to manage incoming and outgoing emails in OpenERP directly,

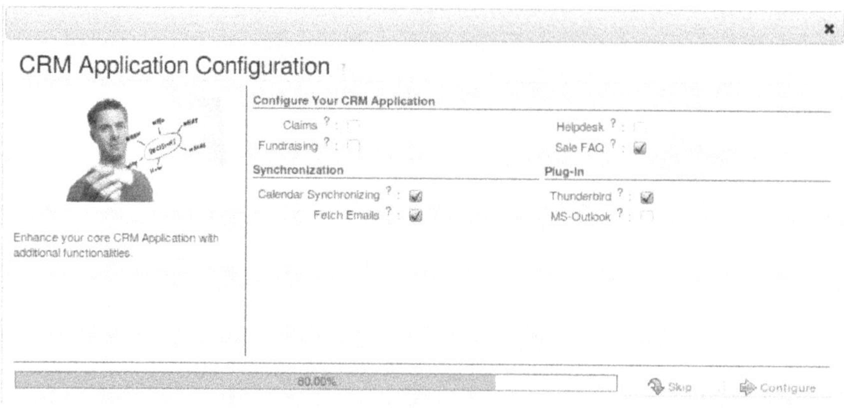


Figure 1.5: *Selecting CRM Configuration*

- `Thunderbird` or `Outlook` according to the email client you are using, to link your current mailbox to OpenERP and to create new leads or partners in OpenERP, directly from your mailbox.

If you have selected all of the above options, the following Configuration Wizards will appear:

- Configure your *Sales* application: click `Configure` to accept the default settings (no options checked).
- Configure your *Knowledge* application: click `Configure` to accept the default settings.
- *Thunderbird / Outlook* Plug-in Configuration: for now, you only have to click the `Save as` button to save the plug-in to your disk (or desktop). Then you can click `Configure` to continue the installation.
- Configure your *Accounting* application: click `Configure` to accept the default settings.
- Configure your *Sales* application: click `Configure` to accept the default settings.
- *Knowledge* application configuration: click `Next` to accept the default settings for the server address.

**Plug-ins**

For the configuration of the plug-in, please refer to the settings in chapter *Managing your CRM from Mozilla Thunderbird* (page 61) or *Managing your CRM from Microsoft Outlook* (page 56).

OpenERP's menu will be displayed, because your system is now ready for actual configuration. To get started, you click the Sales button in OpenERP's main screen. In the next chapter *Adapting OpenERP to your Sales Organization* (page 43) you will start working in the CRM application by telling OpenERP how your company's sales teams are organized.

As your business is growing and evolving all the time, your requirements as to the use of OpenERP are likely to change. To sustain your growth, you can easily extend your CRM with other OpenERP business applications, such as logistics or HR, to name some. OpenERP offers this flexibility; you can start with one business application, such as Customer Relationship Management, and gradually complete OpenERP to suit your ever changing needs!

# Complete Example: from Lead to Sales Order

# 2

In this chapter, we will show you a complete sales flow, from lead to opportunity to quotation to sales order in a step-by-step scenario.

First you will get an explanation about the use case (what Thomas or one of his colleagues is supposed to do). Then the *Notes* will learn you how Thomas (or a colleague of his) enters the information in OpenERP CRM. For the simplicity of the use case, we will do all of the steps under the Admin user.

**Simplified or Extended View**

In OpenERP your user interface will look slightly different according to the User Preferences. In `Simplified` view, the screens will only show the most important fields / tab pages. To see also the fields for the more advanced users, you should switch to the `Extended` view. You can easily switch from *Simplified* to *Extended* view by changing your *User Preferences* through the 'Edit Preferences´ button. For this use case, please switch to ´Extended´ view.

1. Create a new campaign

Your company is exhibiting at the "House & Design" Fair in Paris and Thomas, a salesman of your company, meets lots of prospects during this event. Because Luc, the Sales Manager, would like to know the return on investment from hiring a stand at this fair, he asks Thomas, who will be hosting this event, to make a "House & Design" campaign.

**Campaign**

To create a new campaign, Thomas goes to *Sales → Configuration → Sales → Campaigns* and clicks the *New* button. In the *Campaign Name* field, he types *House & Design*.

2. Create and qualify a new lead

Thomas has to enter all contacts he met at the House & Design Fair as a new lead (contacts, prospects), assigning each individual lead to the "House & Design" campaign. He will start by adding a lead for Mr. John Doe of the *The Interior Design Company* who is interested in redecorating his office.

Figure 2.1: *Campaign*

**Leads**

To create a new lead, Thomas goes to *Sales* → *Leads* and clicks the *New* button. The subject of a lead is in blue, because it is a mandatory field, so Thomas enters *Potential interior design customer* in that field. He uses the *Notes* field to add more information about the lead. When saving the lead, it will be in Draft state. Thomas opens it for further follow-up. In the chapter *Managing your Leads* (page 33) you will find more details about lead creation.

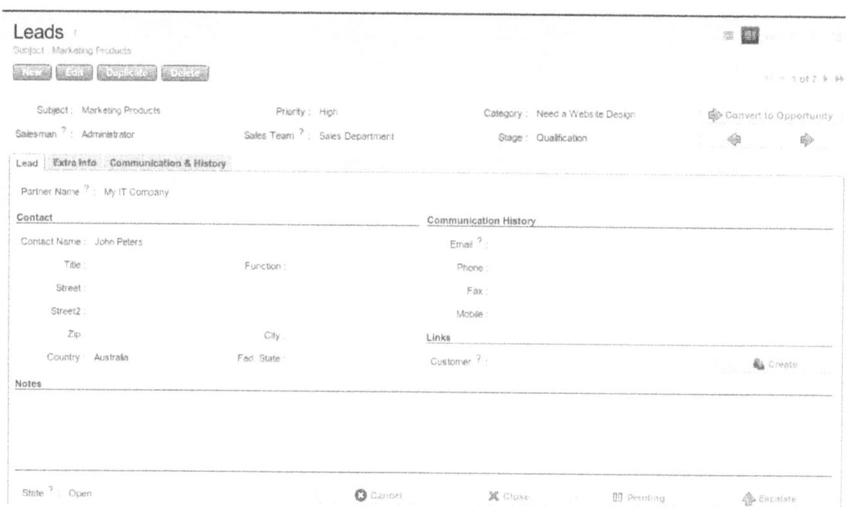


Figure 2.2: *Example of a Lead*

To contact his leads after the Fair and check if any of them can be qualified as a business opportunity, Thomas would like to group his leads by the "House & Design" Campaign, to have an overview of all the leads generated through this campaign.

**Group by**

To group his leads by campaign, Thomas goes to *Sales* → *Leads* and clicks the *Group by* list to show the buttons he can use. He clicks the *Campaign* button and notices that no lead is visible, but only the various campaigns. Each campaign has an arrow in front; he clicks the arrow to display all the leads for that campaign.

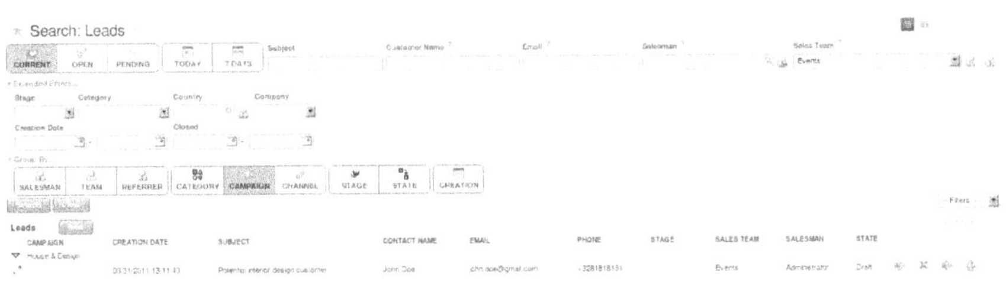


Figure 2.3: *Leads grouped by Campaign*

3. Convert the lead into an opportunity and create a new customer

Because the lead for John Doe from *The Interior Design Company* looks promising, Thomas decides to convert it into an opportunity and at the same time add a new Customer to the company's address book.

On the business opportunity, the salesman should provide more information, such as the estimated income. Thomas indicates that the expected revenue would be 5,000.00€, and that the success rate of the opportunity at this stage is 20%.

Thomas sets Luc, the sales manager, as the person responsible to follow up the opportunity. He also sets the date for the next action and describes that he has to call the potential customer to plan a meeting with Luc, the sales manager.

**Convert to Opportunity**

To convert the lead into an opportunity, Thomas goes to *Sales → Sales → Leads* and opens the lead concerned (there are various possibilities to quickly find the lead he needs). Thomas opens the lead and clicks the *Convert to Opportunity* button (he can also do this from the list of leads by clicking the Convert to Opportunity arrow of the lead concerned). OpenERP asks Thomas whether he wants to create a new partner. He confirms by clicking *Continue* to add the new potential customer to your company's address book. Then he clicks *Next* to convert the promising lead into an opportunity. In the *Expected Revenue* field, Thomas types 5,000.00€, and he enters a success rate of 20%. Thomas clicks the *Create Opportunity* button. As a *Next Action Date*, he sets tomorrow's date and in the *Next Action* field he types *Phone customer to plan meeting*.

**Filters**

The *Advanced Search View* provides a very user-friendly filtering mechanism to easily look up desired records from the list.

Usually, a filter view is composed of three elements, the *Filter* buttons at the top, the *Extended Filters* and the *Group by* option.

> These filters are dynamic, so according to filters you apply, extra columns may be added to the view.

You can also easily combine filters; an arrow will be displayed and you will get a structure according to the order in which you clicked the *Filter* buttons.

> Simply by changing the order in which you select your buttons, you will get a completely different filtered view. E.g. select Salesman first, then Campaign or vice versa.

4. Plan a meeting

One day later, Thomas contacts the prospect and convinces him to meet Luc so that the sales manager can give more information about the product range in view of a quotation.

Thomas plans a meeting for Luc. This meeting is organized next week with the customer and is related to the opportunity. He sets a reminder for Luc.

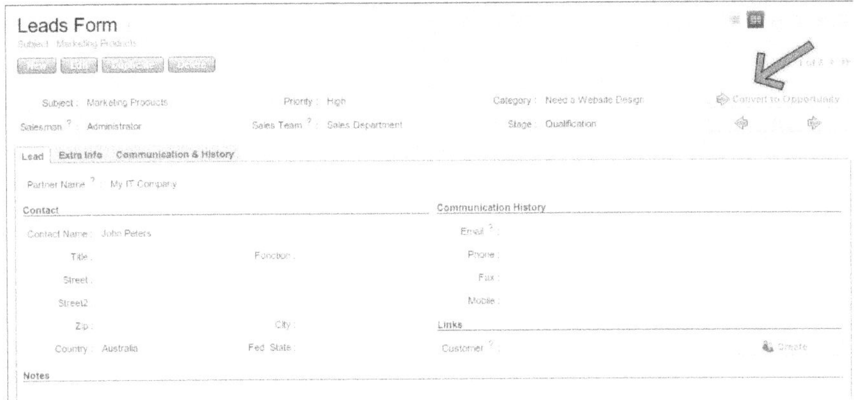


Figure 2.4: *Convert Lead to Opportunity*

**Meeting**

Thomas goes to the list of opportunities through *Sales* → *Sales* → *Opportunities* to check his next actions. He opens the opportunity and contacts John Doe. He enters the key elements of his phone call in the `Details` field. To plan the meeting, Thomas clicks the *Schedule Meeting* button and clicks the *Week* button in the Calendar view. He uses the drag and drop function to schedule the meeting for Luc. He plans the meeting next week from 2 pm to 3 pm. He sets Luc as the person responsible and sets a reminder to be send 2 hours before the start of the meeting. He also changes the `Next Action Date` in the opportunity to the meeting date.

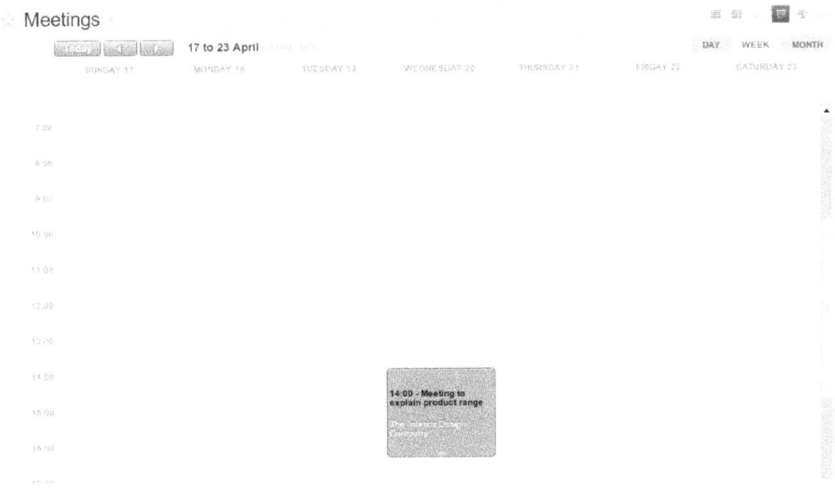


Figure 2.5: *Meeting Calendar*

5. Log an incoming phone call from the customer

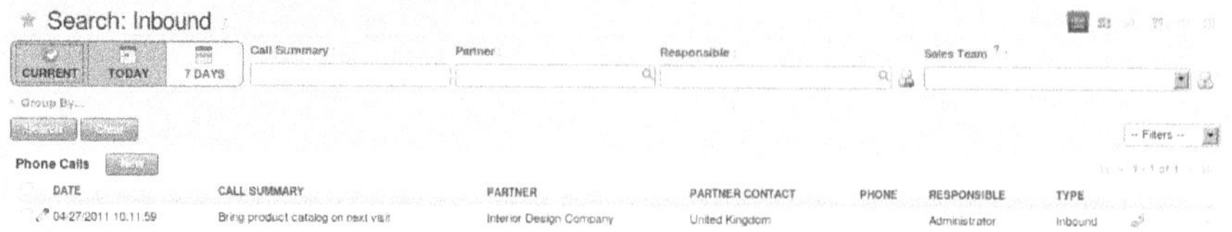


Figure 2.6: *Incoming (Inbound) Call*

A few days later, John Doe calls and Eric, the Product Manager, answers the phone. The customer asks Eric if Luc, the Sales Manager, can bring a product catalog when he comes to see him.

Eric enters a summary of the phone call as an inbound call, and links it to *The Interior Design Company*.

**Phone Calls**

Eric goes to *Sales* → *Sales* → *Phone Calls* and clicks *Inbound*, then *New* to start entering the call. The call can be entered in the line. In the `Call Summary`, he enters *Bring product catalog on next visit* and assigns the call to *The Interior Design Company*. He enters a summary of the phone call in the `Description` field so that Luc knows exactly what has been discussed.

**Call Summary**

Eric can also click the Form view button to open the call form, so that he can add a summary of the phone call in the `Description` field to make sure that Luc knows exactly what has been discussed.

6. Check the history of the customer

To prepare his meeting with *The Interior Design Company*, Luc checks the related customer form to get the history of all related events.

**History**

Luc goes to *Sales* → *Address Book* → *Customers* and types *Interior* in the `Name` field and clicks *Search*. He clicks the customer to open the form. On the *History* tab, Luc gets an overview of all the events, such as meetings and phone calls. So he notices that he has to bring a product catalog to the meeting.

7. Convert the opportunity into a sales quotation

Figure 2.7: *Customer History*

During the meeting, the customer *The Interior Design Company* finally asks to receive a quotation for an Office Desk and Chair. Luc generates the quotation directly from the business opportunity.

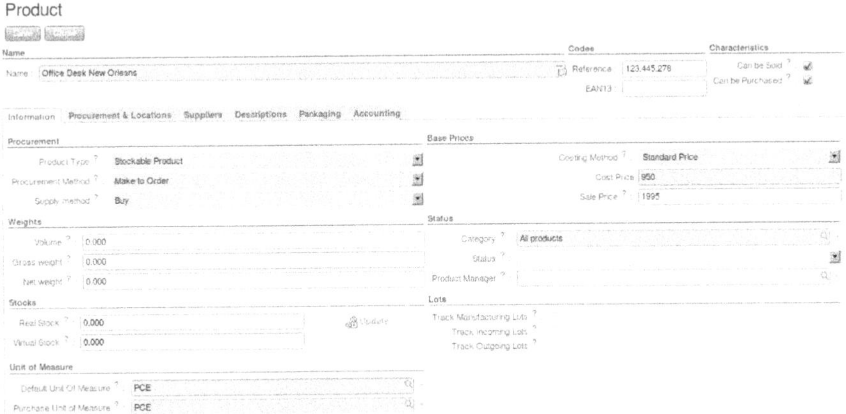


Figure 2.8: *Product*

**Quotation & Products**

Luc opens the opportunity concerned from *Sales → Sales → Opportunities*. He clicks the *Convert to Quote* button, then *Create* to make a quotation that is automatically linked to the opportunity. Now he can enter the products he will be selling. Luc has to create a new product, because the desk ordered is a brand new product. From the sales order line, Luc presses the F1 button in the `Product` field to create a new product. He enters the data as specified in the screenshot. To print the quotation, he clicks *Quotation / Order* in the *Reports* section at the right side of the screen.

8. Check the pipeline of revenues for the next months

Luc, the Sales Manager, would also like to check the quality of his sales team, and he would like to know the delay to close the opportunity. He would like to see the average closing time for the House & Design campaign.

**Average Closing Time**

From the *Sales → Reporting → Opportunities Analysis*, Luc finds the average time taken to successfully respond to a request from a customer in the *Delay to Close* field. Instead of using the default grouping by salesman, Luc clicks the Salesman button in the Group by list to no longer group by salesman, and then he clicks the *Campaign* button to group by campaign.

9. Convert the quotation into a sales order

After some discussion about the prices, the customer decides to sign a contract. Luc confirms the quotation to turn it into a sales order.

**Sales Orders**

Luc opens the quotation concerned from *Sales → Sales Orders*. He clicks the *Quotation* button to see no confirmed sales orders. He opens the quotation by clicking the pencil in front of it, and changes the prices. Then he clicks the *Confirm Order* button to turn the quotation into a sales order. To print the sales order, he clicks *Quotation / Order* in the *Reports* section at the right side of the screen.

Below you find a graphical representation of the sales flow we explained before; the part from quotation to sales order. This view is available in OpenERP. You can open this *Process view* by clicking the question mark next to the *Sales Order* title.

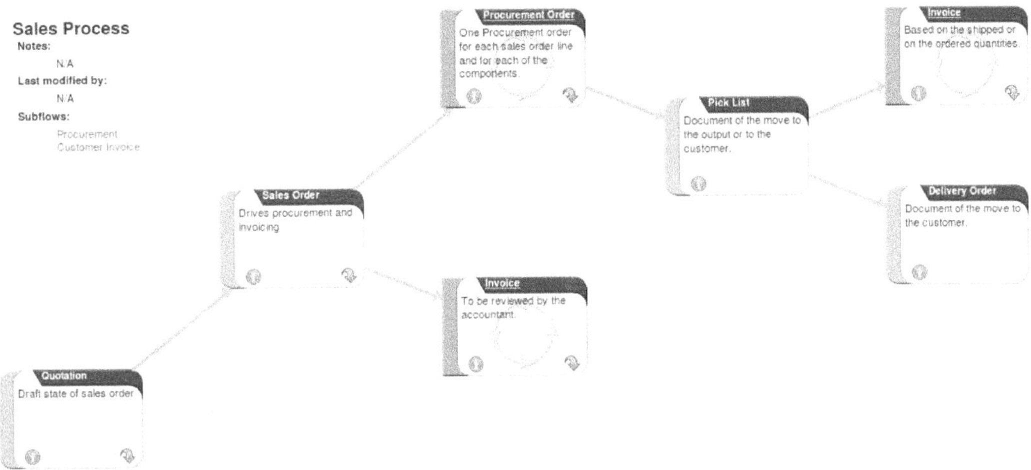


Figure 2.9: *From Quotation to Invoice*

Figure 2.10: *View Buttons*

Before going to the next chapter, just a quick word about the different View buttons in OpenERP. The screenshot below shows the kinds of buttons available. Each button represents a different way of looking at data.

From the opportunities screen, Thomas will click the first *List* view button to get an overview of several opportunities at a time. When Thomas wants more information about a specific opportunity, he will switch to *Form* view. Then Thomas decides he wants to see the opportunities in a graphical representation, so he clicks the *Graph* (3rd) button to display a graph with the opportunities expressed according to Category versus Expected Revenue. He could choose to display the opportunities in *Calendar* view. Thomas wants to see his meetings in a bar chart representation, and so he clicks the *Gannt* view button. To see a process representation of his marketing campaign, he clicks the *Diagram* view button.

Please note that this is just an explanation of the different view buttons.

# Part II

# Managing Customer Acquisition

# Managing your Address Book 3

What is the difference between a partner and a contact in OpenERP? A `Partner` represents an entity that you do business with - a customer, a prospect, or even an employee of your company. In other CRM applications, a partner is also referred to as an Account. A `Contact` represents a person who works for a partner.

Each partner can have an unlimited number of contacts. OpenERP also allows you to have several contacts with the same address type for one partner. You can easily link several Invoice addresses to a customer, for instance.

**Address Types**

If you have recorded several contacts for the same partner, you can tell OpenERP which contact will be used in various documents (e.g. a quotation) by specifying the `Address Type`.

For example, a partner (*company*) can have a delivery address that differs from the company's invoice address. If the Address Types are correctly assigned, OpenERP can automatically select the appropriate address during the creation of the document – an invoice is addressed to the contact that has been assigned the Address Type of Invoice, otherwise to the Default address.

The concept of a partner in OpenERP is much more flexible than in many other management applications. Why is that? Because a partner can be your supplier and your customer at the same time. As a consequence, any data you update for that partner will apply to both customer and supplier! Thanks to this, you no longer need to update your address book several times (or even in several places) for the same partner.

The partner form contains information about the company, such as its corporate name, its primary language, and whether the company is a `Customer` and/or a `Supplier` . The partner form is composed of several tabs.

- the *General* tab contains information about different contacts of that partner, postal information, communication information and the categories the partner belongs to,
- the *Sales & Purchases* tab contains information such as the default salesman and sales team, and the website,
- the *History* tab gives visibility on the complete `Communication History` (meetings, marketing campaign activities, leads and opportunities, phone calls, emails) with the partner. The events the partner has been involved in are created automatically by different documents like phone calls, leads, meetings,
- the *Notes* tab is an area for free text notes.

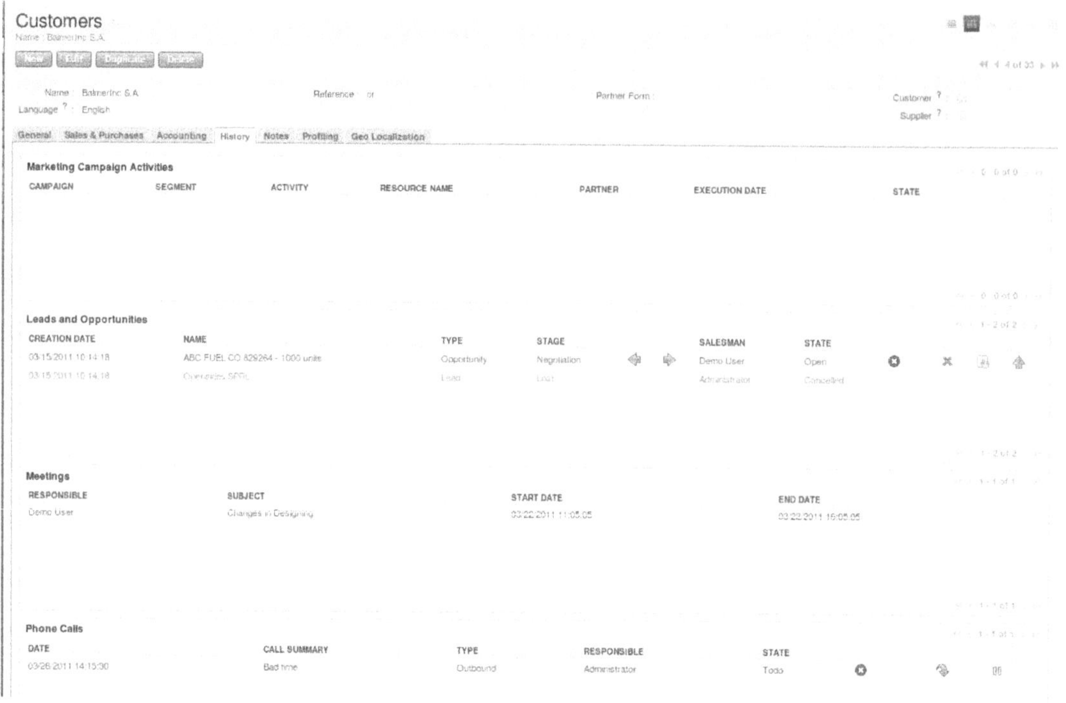


Figure 3.1: *The History Tab of a Customer*

## 3.1 Creating and Updating Partners

Before explaining you how to create a partner, just a quick word on the different ways of representing partners in OpenERP. *List* view shows a list of customers (the default representation when you click the Customers menu). In this view, you can see several customers at a time. *Form* view is displayed when you click a specific customer to start editing or when you create a new customer.

To create a new partner (a company, customer, supplier, ...) or to display the list of existing customers, use the menu *Sales → Address Book → Customers*. This menu does not only allow you to create a new partner, but also to search for partners.

**Mandatory**

Blue fields are always mandatory, meaning that you have to enter a value there. It is impossible to save changes as long as a blue field is not completed.

You should at least enter the company's `Name` in the partner form. Some fields are text fields, other fields may be linked to existing data that have been entered elsewhere, such as `Countries`.

Create a customer with the following data:

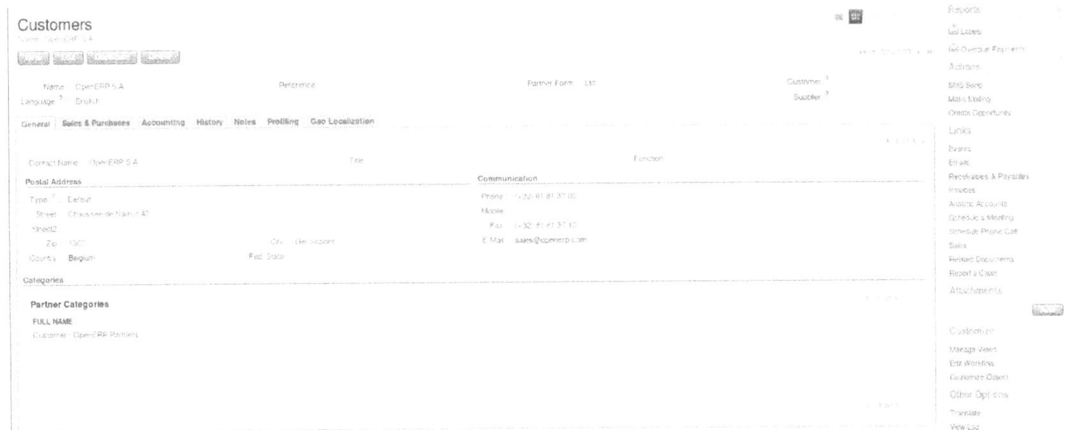


Figure 3.2: *A Customer Form*

- *Name* : `Smith and Offspring`,
- *Customer* checkbox : `checked`,
- *Supplier* checkbox : `unchecked`,
- *Contact Name* : `Stephen Smith`,
- *Type* : `Default`, in the Postal Address section,
- *Save* the form.

**Email**

If you use the email gateway, the Outlook or the Thunderbird plugin, do not forget to register an email addresses to each contact, so that the gateway will automatically attach incoming emails to the right partner.

To update a partner, open the corresponding form, select *Edit* and change the required fields. As explained before, when a company is both one of your customers and a supplier, you just have to edit the partner form once to have changes applied to both customer and supplier.

**Checkboxes**

Why is it important for you to correctly set the Customer and Supplier checkboxes in the partner form? These checkboxes are designed to enable OpenERP to quickly select the partners who should be displayed in some drop-down boxes. An example: when you select a partner in a Sales Quotation, OpenERP will only allow you to select from the list of Customers. And that is precisely what the Customer checkbox is used for.

## 3.2 Managing your Contacts & Addresses

You can have several contacts for one partner. Contacts represent company employees that you are in touch with, along with their address details. For each address you can indicate the type (`Default`, `Invoice`, `Delivery`, `Contact` or `Other`).

Contacts can be entered into the *General* tab of the **Customer** form, or from the list of addresses in the *Sales* → *Address Book* → *Addresses* menu.

**Same Contact, Different Partners**

Do you have contacts who work for several companies, and need to be linked to several partners? Check out the *An Alternative to Manage your Contacts* (page 29) chapter.

## 3.3 Customizing Partner Fields

OpenERP also allows you to customize the `Partner` view to your needs. Click the *Manage Views* option if you want to add fields, delete fields or change the order of fields in a view.

Let us add the `Birthday` field to a contact, in the *Addresses* form view. To do so, go to the *Sales* → *Address Book* → *Addresses* menu and open any address in Form view. In the right menu bar, click *Manage Views*, then *Edit* because the corresponding view will already be preselected.

Go to the last line of the view and click the blue plus (+) sign to add a field to the *Communication* group. Proceed as in the figure below, then click the *Update* button.

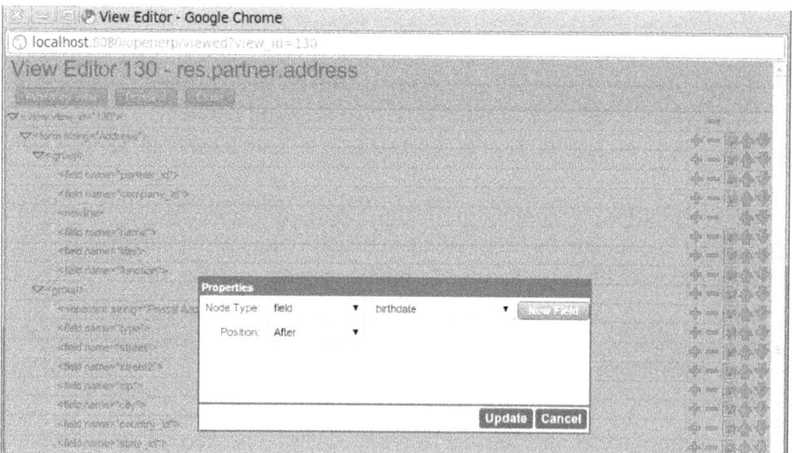


Figure 3.3: *Add the Birthday Field for a Contact*

In the *Properties* screen that appears, you can change the label to `Birthday` in the `String` field. To indicate that a new field can be used in the corresponding search view, make sure to select `Always`

`Searchable`. Click the *Update* button to confirm your changes. Click *Preview* to see your result. The `Birthday` field will now appear in your *Address* form view, ready to be used.

## 3.4 Performing Actions on Customers

At the right side of the *Customers* list or form view, you will find a list of all of the reports, actions and links available for the selected partner(s). You can perform actions and print reports both from List and from Form view, List view allowing you to do actions for several partners at the same time.

**Actions**

To display the list of possible actions, just select one or more customers or click the arrow at the top of the right side bar.

You can create a new opportunity for a customer, or start a mass mailing. Mass mailings will usually be started from list view, because you will select several partners at a time.

**Campaigns**

For mass mailings, you might prefer to use the Direct Marketing application, which offers great functionality (please refer to chapter *Driving your Marketing Campaigns* (page 77)).

Another action enables you to quickly send an SMS message.

**Send an SMS message**

To send an SMS message from standard Open ERP you will have to place an order with the bulk SMS gateway operator Clickatell™ http://clickatell.com.

To send an SMS message to a partner or a selection of several partners, first select the partners in list view, then click the *SMS Send* Action icon.

## 3.5 Finding your Partners using Filters

Open the *Customers* list view to discover the search options allowing you to easily filter your partners. You can group by `Salesman` to see which customers have already been assigned a salesman or not. Click the button at the right (the icon of the person) to see the customers you are responsible for.

**Limit**

If you want to display more than the 20 partners displayed by default, click the `1 to 20 of - XX` option at the bottom of the screen to be able to change the limit.

Filters also allow you to quickly set lists of customers for which you want to do specific actions. Through the `New Filter` option, you can also add your own filters for any field related to the `Customer` form.

**Filters**

You can easily create your own frequently used filters by prefiltering the data the way you want and then using the Save Filter option.

## 3.6 Categorizing your Partners

OpenERP uses categories to organize all of its partners according to their relationship with your company (customer, prospect, supplier, and so on). Each partner may be attached to several categories. To open the list of available partner categories, use the menu *Sales → Configuration → Address Book → Partner Categories*.

Click one of the categories in the partner category structure to get a list of the partners in that category. If you click a category that has subcategories, you will get a list of all of the partners in the main category and in all of its subcategories.

**Categories**

To create a new category, go to the menu *Sales → Configuration → Address Book → Partner Categories* and click the *New* button.

Because categories can be organized according to a tree structure, you can apply an action at any level of the structure: a marketing promotion activity, for example, can be applied either to all customers, or selectively only to customers in one category and its subcategories.

You can create your own categories and assign them to your partner from the *Customer* form. Another way of assigning the corresponding partner to a category is to open the category from the *Partner Categories*.

In the *Profiling your Customers* (page 93) chapter, you will see how to assign partners to categories automatically using segmentation rules.

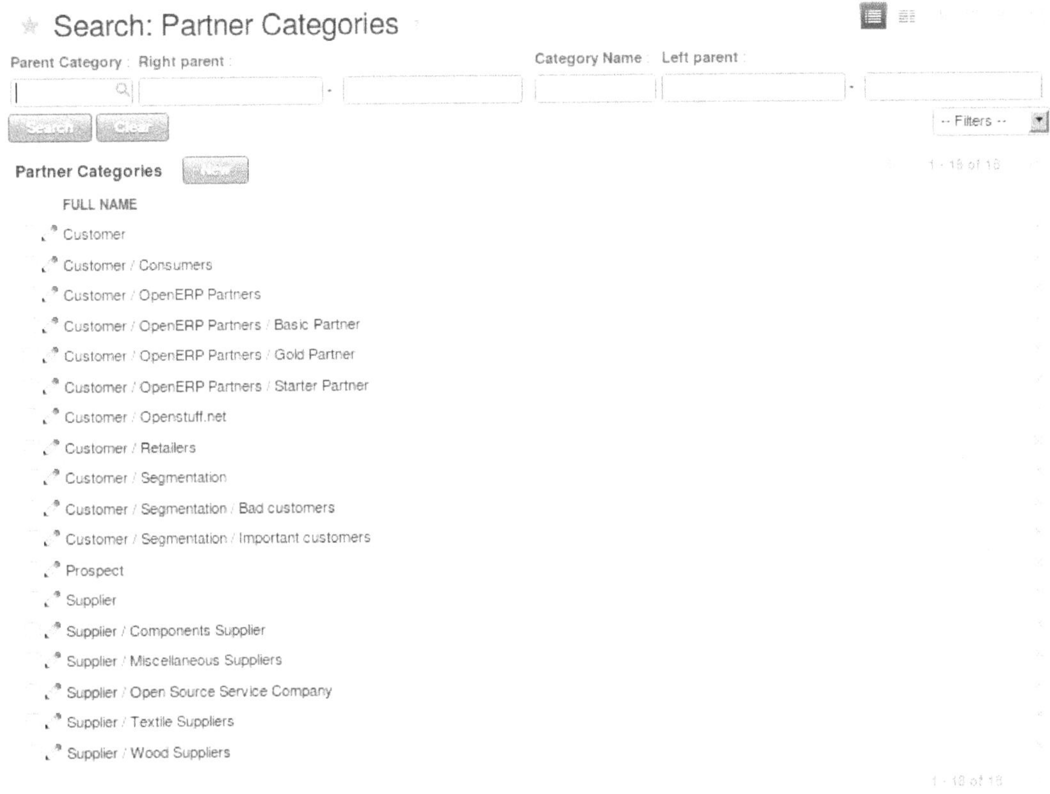


Figure 3.4: *List of Partner Categories*

## 3.7 An Alternative to Manage your Contacts

According to your kind of business, the standard way of linking several contacts to one partner may not be flexible enough for you. You could perfectly well have the same employees working for several of your companies. Or maybe you work with representatives ensuring follow up of several of your customers. So you would want to have the same contact linked to different partners.

Of course, OpenERP provides an alternative, the `base_contact` module, which gives you even more flexibility in managing your contacts.

Easily share the same contact (an employee, for instance), who may perfectly have different jobs, with several partners. You only need to enter (or *create*) the contact once and link it to the partners concerned, while specifying the position the contact holds for each company in particular. Any changes to contact information only need to be made once for them to be applied to all partners the contact is related to!

We illustrate the concept of multiple relationships between contacts and partners (companies) through an example. The figure *Advanced Contact Management* (page 30) shows two companies having several addresses (places of business) and several contacts attached to these addresses.

In this example you will find the following elements:

- The ABC bank has two places of business, represented by the addresses of ABC Belgium and ABC Luxembourg,
- The addresses of Dexey France and Dexey Belgium belong to the Dexey company,
- At the office of ABC Luxembourg, you have the contacts of the director (D. Smith) and the accountant (A. Doe),
- Mr Doe holds the post of accountant for ABC Luxembourg and Dexey France,
- Mr D. Smith is director of Dexey France and Dexey Belgium and we also have his private address which is not attached to a partner.

An extra menu option will be added, allowing you to display the list of contacts, through *Sales → Address Book → Contacts.*

The screenshot below illustrates how contacts are handled with the advanced Contacts configuration.

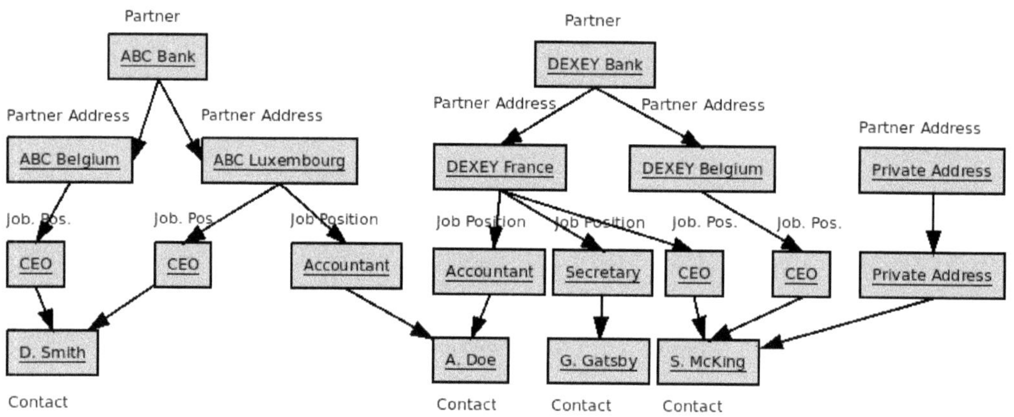


Figure 3.5: *Advanced Contact Management*

This is a clear way to illustrate the complexities that may be accomplished in OpenERP.

If you correct or change a contact name in the contact form, the changes will be applied to all the posts occupied in the different companies.

The screen below represents a partner form. You can add several addresses, such as Invoice & Delivery, and a list of contacts per address. Each contact has its own data, such as name, function, phone number and email.

Go to *Sales → Address Book → Contacts* to open a contact form. You enter data in the contact form, containing information such as mobile phone, different functions occupied, and personal blog. You can also add a photo of your contact. If you click the *Functions and Addresses* line, you will get more details about the job (such as start date, end date and fax).

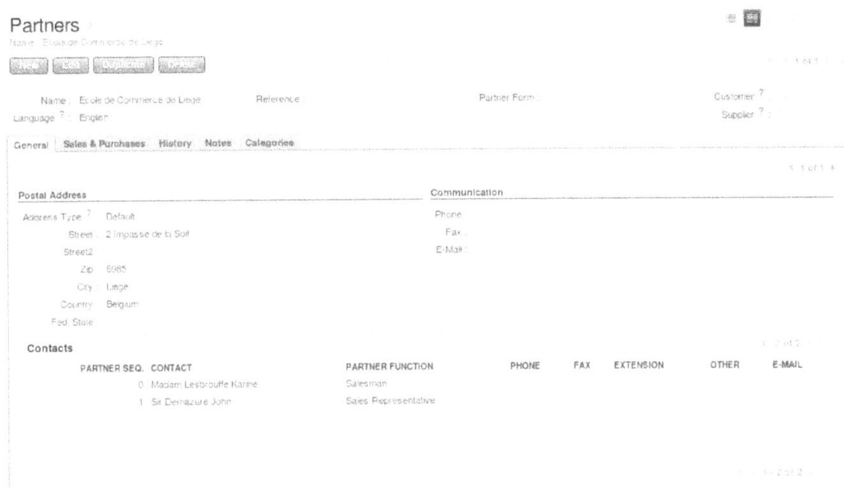


Figure 3.6: *Partner Form with the Advanced Contacts Management*

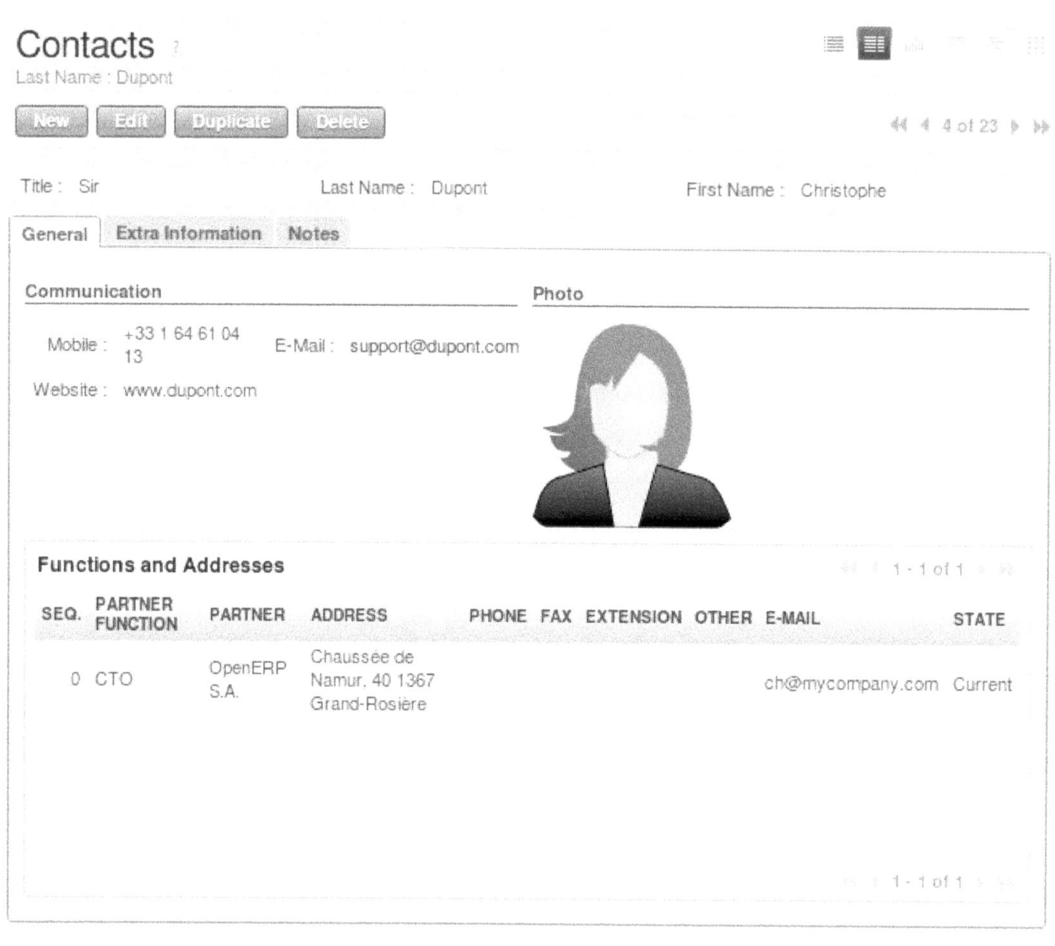


Figure 3.7: *Detail of a Position occupied by a Contact at a Partner*

# 4 Managing your Leads

To define leads, imagine a bucket full of potential sales contacts expressing an interest in your company's products.

A lead represents a potential customer with whom you have not established a relationship yet. Usually a lead contains valuable information to realise future sales opportunities. However, the most common mistake is that such key information too often gets lost, because it is registered nowhere. And even when registered, it might still be difficult to track any activity for that lead, because the information is not at hand when you need it.

Storing leads information in a central place such as OpenERP will release you of these worries.

So when would you create a lead in OpenERP, either manually or automatically? The following events could be a trigger:

- An inquiry email sent to one of your company's generic email addresses, such as sales@mycompany.com, from the mailgateway,
- A business card from a prospective customer met briefly at an exhibition: you have to contact him again to qualify the lead and to know if there is any possibility of a sales opportunity; registered manually,
- A database of potential customers in a given sector and region imported through a CSV file. The potential customers have to be contacted again individually or through a mass mailing to determine which contacts require further follow-up,
- An interesting contact that you met during a business networking event. You have to qualify it before assigning a salesperson to the contact,
- A form completed on your website directly integrated into OpenERP using our webservice. Before converting the form into a sales proposition or opportunity, you should read and handle the person's request.

Employees in the marketing or presales department will usually work on leads. Once these leads will be converted into customers and/or sales opportunities, the sales department pays individual attention to each opportunity. Of course, before converting a lead into an opportunity, some qualification work has to be done.

OpenERP allows you to easily configure the way your company qualifies leads. You can create your own stages through *Sales → Configuration → Leads & Opportunities → Stages*. Use the sequence number to determine the order of the stages, i.e. 10 for First Call, 20 for Renewing Contact and so on. Of course, you can also drag & drop a stage to another place to automatically change the order of all the stages. A salesman can change the status of the lead according to the response from the prospect and enter the result of this contact in the lead form (e.g. in the `Notes` field).

From the *Sales → Sales → Leads* menu, you can qualify each individual lead through the `Stage` field that is found up to the right of the lead definition. To move your lead automatically to the next step from the list of leads, you can use the button that looks like a green, right arrow.

Leads can be assigned to a *Sales Team* for easy follow-up (see *Adapting OpenERP to your Sales Organization* (page 43)). Each user can be added to a default sales team which can be specified in the *User Preferences*. When you define a tree structure for your sales teams, you can also escalate a lead to another sales team for further actions.

**Leads or Opportunities**

Companies may decide to not use leads, but instead to keep all information directly in an opportunity. For some companies, leads are merely an extra step in the sales process. You could call this extended (start from lead) versus simplified (start from opportunity) customer relationship management. OpenERP perfectly allows for either one of these approaches to be chosen. If your company handles its sales from opportunities directly, feel free to move on to chapter *Optimizing your Sales Cycle through Opportunities* (page 41), although most of the features explained below also apply to opportunities.

In the next sections we will explain in more detail some examples of what *Leads* in OpenERP can be used for.

**Leads Menu is not displayed**

In `Simplified` view, `Leads` will not be displayed. To see not also opportunities, but also leads, you should switch to the `Extended` view. You can easily switch from *Simplified* to *Extended* view by changing your *User Preferences* through the *Edit Preferences* button.

## 4.1 Storing your Business Cards effectively

Potential customers are usually entered as a lead in the system. This means that you do not create a partner or a sales opportunity until you have qualified whether the lead is interesting or not.

**Qualification**

When a qualified lead requires further actions, you can turn the lead into a partner and, eventually, a sales opportunity.

To make a new lead, go to the *Sales → Sales → Leads* menu and click the *New* button. In the **Lead** form that opens, you can enter the contact data of this new potential customer and add notes.

You can also set the status of a lead according to the qualification work that has been carried out:

- `Draft` : the lead data have been entered, no work has been done yet and a salesperson has not yet been assigned to the request,

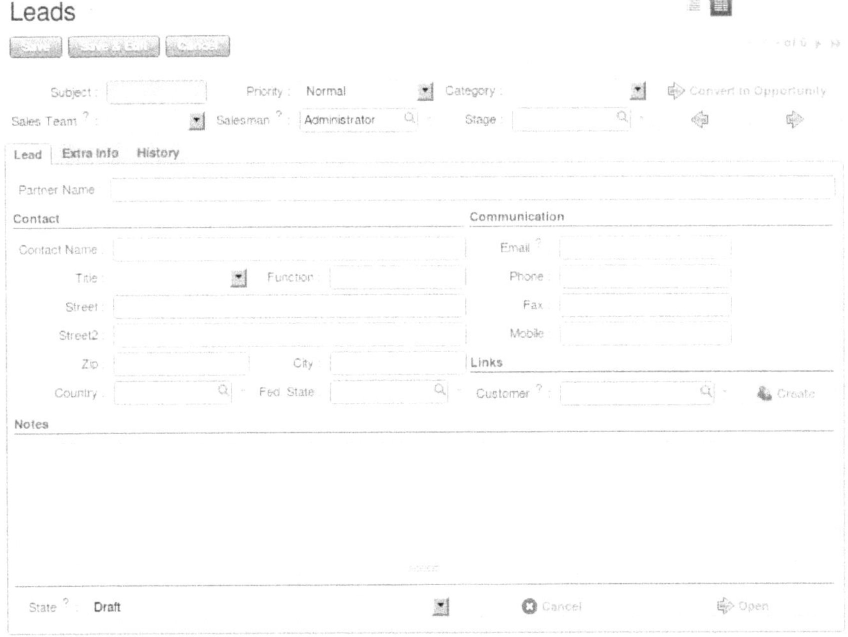


Figure 4.1: *Creating a New Lead*

- `Open`: the lead is being handled,
- `Closed`: the lead has been converted into a partner and/or a sales opportunity,
- `Pending`: the lead is waiting for a response from the potential customer,
- `Escalate`: the lead is escalated to the upper sales team in the tree structure for further actions,
- `Cancelled`: the lead has been cancelled because the salesperson has decided that it is not worth following up.

A lead status can easily be changed, even from list view (the standard view when you start the **Leads** program). Simply click the green arrows to change the status of a lead.

On the *Extra* tab in the **Leads** form, you find statistics about days to open and close and more information about the campaign, the channel, and so on.

On the *Communication & History* tab in the **Leads** form, you can see a complete history of all actions regarding this lead. You can also add internal notes and change the status of a lead while adding such a note. Send an email directly from the lead simply by clicking the *Send New Email* button (to configure your email settings, please refer to chapter *Communication Tools* (page 53). You can add attachments to internal notes and emails you send to the prospect. You can customize your message and have the status changed after an email has been sent; you could automatically have the lead set to **Pending**, because you require a response from the customer before further actions can be taken.

Figure 4.2: *Extra Tab*

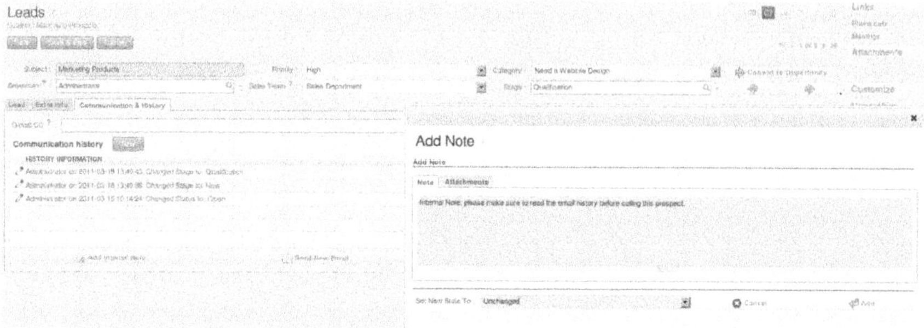


Figure 4.3: *Communication & History Tab*

## 4.2 Importing a Leads Database

You can also import a huge list of leads. That may be useful if you have bought a database of potential prospects that you want to load into OpenERP to handle them all at the same time.

Start with a list of leads in CSV format, for instance. If your prospects database is provided in another format, you can easily convert it to the CSV format using Microsoft Excel or OpenOffice Calc.

**Import**

The best thing to do to make sure your import will go smoothly, first export all the required Lead fields using the *Export* function, and then edit the resulting csv file for import.

Open the **Leads** form using the menu *Sales* → *Sales* → *Leads*. In *Other Options*, click the *Import* link. (You can also import from List view, just open the action window on the right (by clicking the arrow) and in *Other Options*, click the *Import* link.)

Select your file containing the leads information and click *Import File*. OpenERP will automatically map the column headers from your CSV file to the corresponding fields in OpenERP. If necessary, you can click `CSV Options` to change the settings so that they match your local settings.

Check the online chapter about system administration for more information on import and export on http://doc.openerp.com/v6.0/book/.

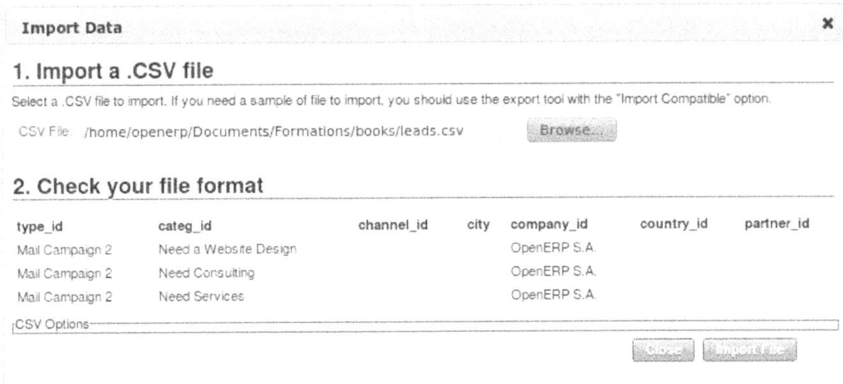


Figure 4.4: *Importing Leads into the System*

> **Various Imports**
>
> Importing and Exporting data in OpenERP is a generic function available to all resources. So you can import and export such lists as partners, opportunities, accounting entries, products and price lists.

Clearly there are other methods of generating leads automatically or semi-automatically:

- Through a Contact Form on your Website;
- Using the Outlook or Thunderbird plugin to insert new leads directly from the salesman's mailbox when he sees promising emails,
- Using the email gateway for each incoming email from a certain address (such as sales@mycompany.com) which may create a lead automatically from the contents of the email.

These different methods are described later in this book (see chapter *Automating your Lead Acquisition* (page 89)).

## 4.3 Organizing Leads

To help the users organize and handle leads efficiently, OpenERP provides several features in the CRM to be used according to the needs of each:

Use the *Sales* → *Sales* → *Leads* view to organize your leads:

- Display a list of all the leads (qualified, open, not open, ...) according to the sales team you are linked to,
- Create a new lead by clicking *New*,

- Display Unassigned Leads, click the button next to the *Salesman* field,
- Display a list of all your leads you still need to handle (your open and draft leads),
- Display a list of all your leads that are waiting for a customer response (usually in *Pending* status). This enables you to check periodically on your work to do,
- Display a list of all the leads assigned to different salespeople,
- Use Extended Filters to display all the leads created today or during the last week, in a specific time period, and so on,
- Quickly find leads not yet assigned to a Campaign, by clicking the Group by button and then Campaign.

The sales manager can use this **Leads** view to easily keep track of what each salesperson is working on.

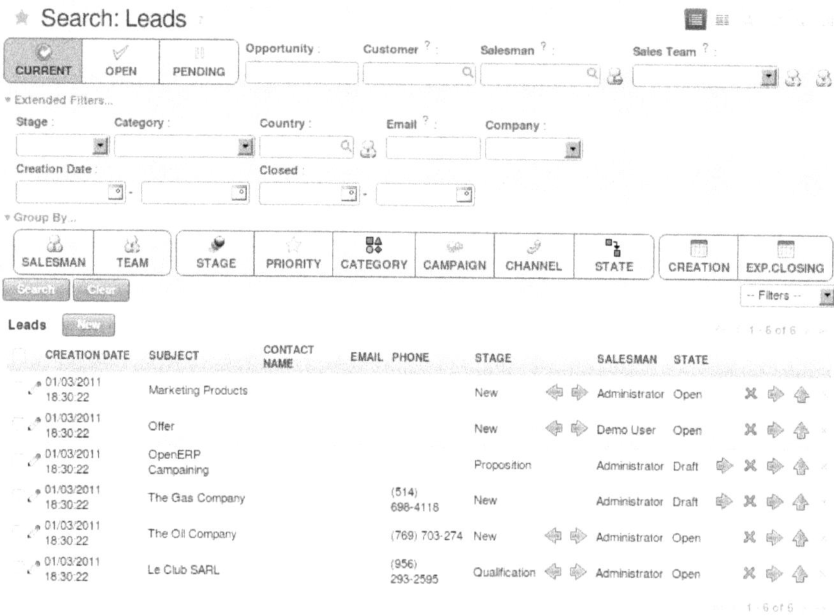

Figure 4.5: *List of Leads to be Handled*

Leads can also be prioritized. Salespeople can assign a priority to their lead, and then start working on their leads from the top of the list, which is sorted by priority.

## 4.4 Analysing Leads

OpenERP also offers statistical reports to keep track of your Lead Management. The *Sales → Reporting → Leads Analysis* report allows you to check various leads-related elements. You can look at processing delays, number of responses given and emails sent (if you use the email gateway feature). Sort your leads analysis by different groups to get accurate, grained analysis.

These are some analysis possibilities of the **Leads Analysis** report.

1. Leads by State and per Month

To analyse the leads by status, group the leads by qualification level (`Stage`) and status (`State`), this can also be done for individual months (first group by `Month`).

2. Leads by Origin

Analyse leads according to their state (open, lost, won) and their stage (e.g. cold / hot or new / qualification / ... ) and find out how many leads belong to each state / stage.

3. How effective are your Campaigns?

Group by Campaign to easily find the number of leads by campaign and the total number of leads. You can also select a specific campaign in your filter.

4. Leads by Priority.

Group by Priority to see which leads are hot, warm or cold.

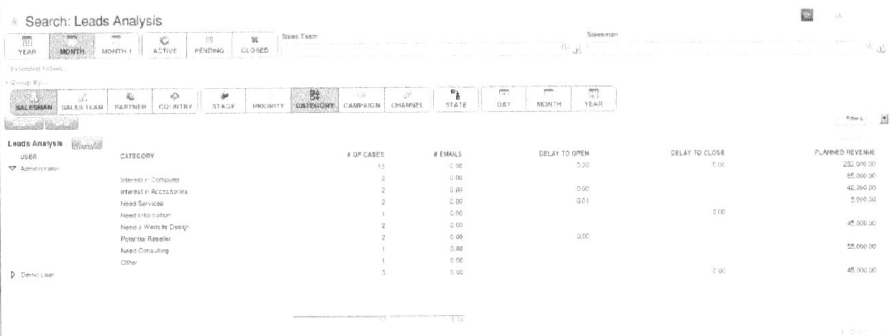


Figure 4.6: *Leads Analysis*

# Optimizing your Sales Cycle through Opportunities 5

While a lead represents the first contact with a prospect yet to be qualified, a sales opportunity represents a potential contract. Each opportunity has to be followed up by a salesperson (or sales team) spending time to qualify the opportunity, and this either by making a quotation or canceling the opportunity.

Leads are generally handled by the dozen, with the automation of certain responses or emails. Opportunities, on the contrary, are usually tracked one by one by the salespeople, because an opportunity involves a negotiation process with the customer to be.

Just like for leads, OpenERP provides specific features to handle sales opportunities efficiently. All opportunities can be found in the menu *Sales → Sales → Opportunities*.

With opportunities, you can manage and keep track of your sales pipeline by creating specific customer- or prospect-related sales documents to follow up potential sales. Information such as expected revenue, opportunity stage, expected closing date, communication history, next action date, next action, and much more can be stored.

Opportunities can be connected to the email gateway: new emails may create opportunities, each of them automatically gets the history of the conversation with the customer. You and your sales team(s) will be able to plan meetings and phone calls from opportunities, convert them into quotations, manage related documents, track all customer-related activities, and much more.

**Attachments**

By default, you can keep attachments in OpenERP to make sure all linked documents are directly accessible. At the right side of the screen, under `Attachments`, click the *Add* button to start linking documents to your opportunity. With the *Browse* button, you can search for the file to be attached in your directories. You can add attachments in the same way for leads, for instance. If you also want those documents to be indexed (not for pictures), you should install the Knowledge Application.

## 5.1 Converting Leads into Customers or Opportunities

If the salesperson thinks that the lead has been well qualified and that there is a real opportunity, following the contact he had with the prospect, he can easily convert the lead into a partner / opportunity using the button *Convert to Opportunity*.

Clicking the *Convert to Opportunity* button offers several possibilities, allowing you also to avoid duplicate partners:

- You can decide to just create the opportunity and keep the contact data from the lead without creating a partner,

- You can convert to an opportunity, and create a new partner if it does not exist yet, or merge the contact with an existing partner,
- You first create a partner, and later you convert the lead to an opportunity.

To create only a partner, click the button *Create* next to the `Customer` field. You can also decide to add the contact data of the lead as a new contact to an existing partner.

OpenERP shows a window allowing you to select:

- whether you want to create a new partner,
- whether you want to link this contact to an existing partner (merge).

OpenERP opens a partner form containing the information from the lead. At this stage you can complete the contact details or add any other information for the partner.

The partner created is automatically attached to the lead, which enables you to keep complete traceability from the lead. To find this information, you should take a look at the *Communication & History* tab in the lead.

Instead, you can also combine the step of creating a partner and directly the lead converting into an opportunity through the *Convert to Opportunity* feature.

**Convert to Opportunity**

When you click the *Convert to Opportunity* button and the email address of the new contact is filled out, OpenERP will check whether this email address corresponds to an email address of an existing partner. If so, OpenERP will directly propose to merge the new contact with the partner found.

When you click the *Convert to Opportunity* button and the partner already exists, OpenERP opens a window allowing you to select:

- whether you want to create a new opportunity,
- whether you want to add this lead to an existing opportunity (merge).

OpenERP shows the title of the opportunity (taken from the lead description) and the partner. Make sure to enter the estimated revenue and the success rate (probability) of converting to a sales.

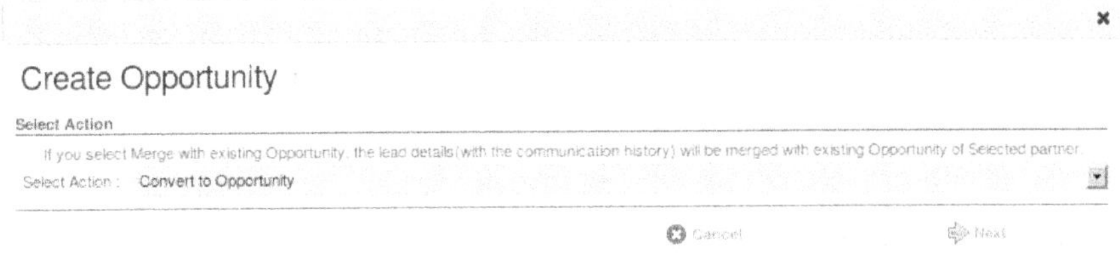


Figure 5.1: *Converting a Lead into a Sales Opportunity*

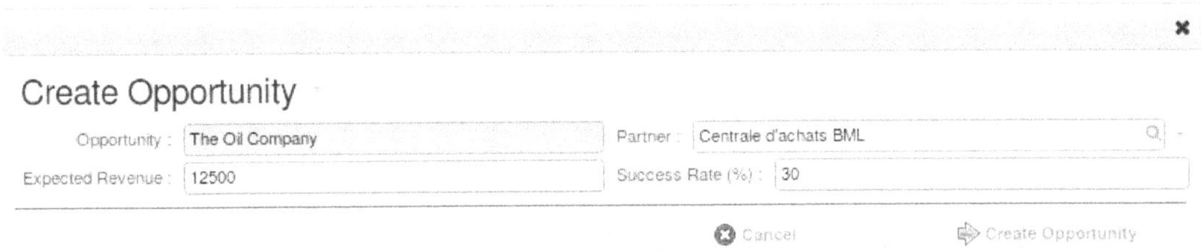


Figure 5.2: *From Lead to Opportunity: Details*

## 5.2 Adapting OpenERP to your Sales Organization

Your sales organization may be composed of several groups which for instance address different customer segments or geographies, sell different products and services and often manage different sales cycles. As a manager you will want to track the performance not only for each individual but also for each group.

OpenERP allows you to do that by defining *Sales Teams*. A sales team is a group of sales people who are performing a similar position. Implementing sales teams is a powerful tool. It allows you to:

- Assign leads or opportunities according to their nature to a sales team first. Then according to the company's policy, the opportunities can be assigned to a given individual. For example opportunities can be assigned to a *Western Region sales team* or *Eastern Region sales team* in the first place according to their location. Each sales person may pick unassigned opportunities in his sales team according to his availability,
- You can group your sales teams according to a tree structure (hierarchy). This allows you to have a view of your sales activity at different granular levels (local, regional, national for instance),
- Some sales teams may manage their opportunities through different sales cycles. For instance a car dealership which addresses both the residential and corporate customers, will have different sales cycles.
- For each sales team, you can assign a responsible user and an email address that will be used when creating or replying to emails from OpenERP. This will be proposed by default in OpenERP when you create an event for this customer.

> **Sales Teams**
>
> To define your Sales Teams, go to *Sales → Configuration → Sales → Sales Teams*.

Let us take the example of a bank to explain how you can define your sales teams. A bank has several departments, such as Insurance, Accounts, Assets, Credit Management. Each department may be divided into several subdepartments. For Insurance, this could be Group Insurance and Home Insurance. The hierarchical structure of your Sales Teams could then be as follows:

- **Insurance Sales Team**
  - Group Insurance
  - Home Insurance
- Accounts Sales Team
- Assets Sales Team
- Credit Management Sales Team

## 5.3 Defining the Key Steps of your Sales Cycle

Each company will have similar, yet customized stages to qualify opportunities.

To see & define stages for Opportunity qualification, go to *Sales → Configuration → Opportunities → Stages*.

The key steps of your Sales Cycle are what OpenERP calls `Stages`. You can use the stages to improve your sales capacity, because they allow you to find out the reasons why deals succeed or fail.

Stages will allow salesmen to easily track where a specific opportunity is positioned in the sales cycle. One of the frequent difficulties in using stages is that different sales people may assess differently in which stage their sales opportunity should be. You can avoid this by clearly stating what you expect as a result for each stage. This way, your sales teams will use the same stages throughout the qualification process, allowing the sales manager to get accurate and consistent information. We also recommend to limit the number of stages in your sales cycle to make them easy to follow up.

As you progress in your sales cycle, and move from one stage to another, you can expect to have more precise information about a given opportunity. For example, when setting an opportunity as 'Qualified', you may decide that the salesman has to enter the "Expected Revenue" and the "Expected Closing Date." You can also have the probability changed automatically when changing stages, by selecting the "Change Probability Automatically" checkbox. If checked, OpenERP will set the probability of the opportunity to the probability defined in the stage. If you set a probability of 0% (Lost) or 100% (Won), OpenERP will assign the corresponding stage when the opportunity is marked as Lost or Won.

As an example, to track your opportunities, you can assign the following stages to the sales team. For each stage, you assume you will define criteria that have to be met prior to moving to the next stage.

1. Territory - Segment your opportunities into territories.
2. Qualified – Attract the prospect's interest, determine whether the prospect has a need.

   **What is the expected result?**

   - The need to buy the product/service has been confirmed,
   - Confirm that there is a budget.

3. Qualified Sponsors – Ask the right questions and listen carefully to identify and thoroughly understand the prospect's needs.

   **What is the expected result?**

   - Current pain points identified,
   - Identify what the prospect wants to achieve,
   - Identify the decision-maker.

3. Proposition – Discuss some solutions to determine the customer's preferences, recommend specific solutions to answer the customer's needs.

   **What is the expected result?**

   - Demo and/or Proposal given,
   - Decision maker confirmed his interest to purchase,
   - Preliminary pricing confirmed/agreed upon.

4. Negotiation – Submit the final proposal to the customer and begin the negotiation process.

   **What is the expected result?**

   - Negotiation concluded,
   - Contract terms/conditions agreed upon,
   - Contract submitted for signature.

5. Won/Lost – Register the final step of the opportunity.

   **What is the expected result?**

   - Contract signed / not signed,
   - Next steps.

You can apply your own stages throughout the qualification process by means of the `Stage` field that is found up to the right of the opportunity definition. To move an opportunity automatically to the next step, you can use the button that looks like a green, right arrow.

OpenERP also has other sales configuration options; you can define your *Campaigns*, allowing you to keep track of the event your leads and opportunities refer to. Examples of campaigns are Google Adwords, an event you are hosting, a newsletter. With *Categories* you identify your prospect's needs (e.g. Needs Training, Needs OpenERP Online), while *Channels* help you to keep visibility on how the lead or opportunity entered the system (email, website, referred by an existing customer).

Figure 5.3: *Example of Opportunity Stages*

## 5.4 Planning your Next Actions

When a lead has been converted into an opportunity, the latter can be assigned to any salesperson. You might designate an opportunity manager in the company who is responsible for assigning the new opportunities to different salespeople according to the job they do, their location or availability.

Of course, OpenERP allows you to automate such steps in your sales cycle. With *Automated Rules* you can tell the system for instance to automatically assign opportunities to a sales person or to change the status of an opportunity according to specific criteria.

**Automated Actions**

To access the CRM rules, use the *Sales* → *Configuration* → *Automated Actions* → *Automated Actions* menu.

Let's give an example of what you can use Automated Actions for. Suppose you want to have OpenERP assign opportunities for customers in the IT Sector category directly to Thomas, your IT salesman. Thomas should be assigned automatically when a lead is converted to an opportunity by clicking the *Convert to Opportunity* button in the *Leads* screen. This can be set through the `Object` field in the *Automated Actions* form; just select *Convert/Merge Opportunity*.

The screenshots below illustrate how you can tell OpenERP to do this automatically for you.

When you answer to an opportunity from the *Communication & History* tab, you can directly have the status of the opportunity changed. You can also add a Global CC, even with multiple email addresses separated by ';'. This ensures that when any email regarding this opportunity is sent, all the persons defined in Global CC will be notified.

Planning your next actions also refers to filling fields or performing actions manually, without interference of automated rules. It is important that you fill all the opportunity fields accurately. To ensure good follow-up and prioritise your opportunities, make sure to register the `Next Action Date` and the `Next Action` in the Opportunity. In the *Opportunities* screen, you can group your search results by these fields, so that you know exactly how to plan your work.

You can use the filters to group by `Priority` and then click the `Next Action Date` column to sort by next action date to easily follow up your opportunities and know exactly what you have to do.

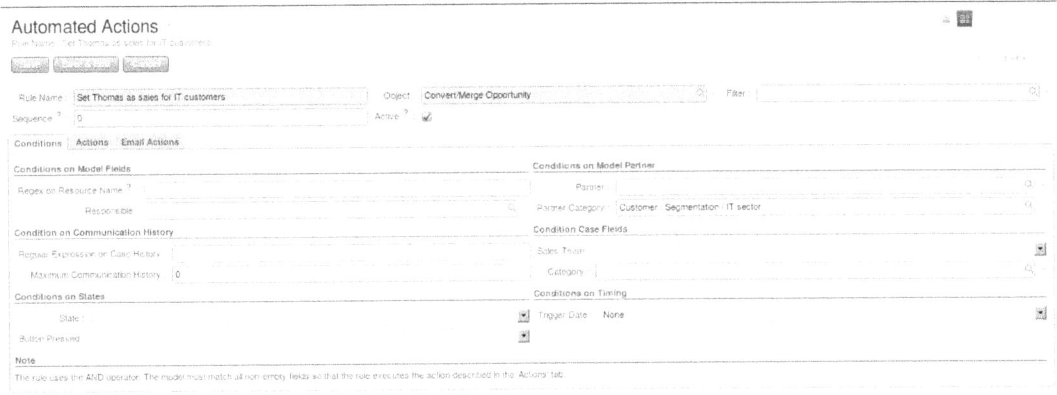


Figure 5.4: *Step 1: Conditions Tab of Automated Actions*

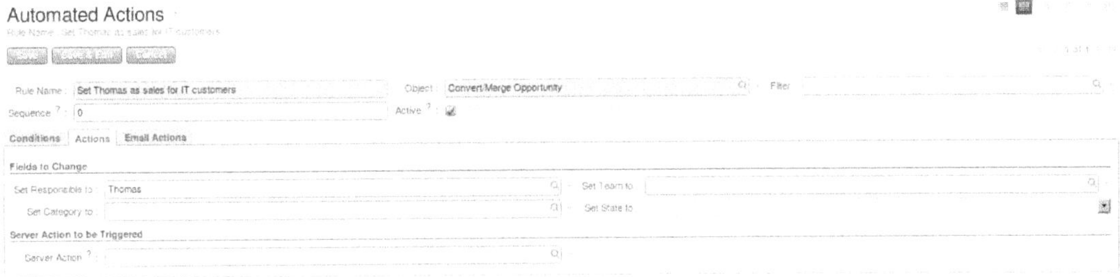


Figure 5.5: *Step 2: Actions Tab of Automated Actions*

## 5.5 Planning your Meetings & Calls Effectively

Planning your meetings & calls does not only allow you to structure your work, but also to improve your sales skills by learning from your call & meeting history. For both Meetings & Calls, you can enter a complete report of what you discuss!

As explained in chapter *Complete Example: from Lead to Sales Order* (page 11), you can schedule a meeting directly from an opportunity. When you create a meeting from an opportunity, related fields will be prefilled from the opportunity. For the ease of reading, Thomas will schedule a new meeting from an opportunity here and set Luc, the Sales Manager, as the person responsible for the meeting. He wants to send Luc a reminder 1 day before the meeting starts.

**Schedule a Meeting from an Opportunity**

To plan the meeting, Thomas clicks the *Schedule Meeting* button in the **Opportunity** and clicks the *Week* button in the Calendar view. He uses the drag and drop function to schedule the meeting for Luc. He plans the meeting next Wednesday from 2 pm to 3 pm. He sets Luc as the person responsible and sets a reminder to be send 1 day before the start of the meeting. He also changes the `Next Action Date` in the opportunity to the meeting date.

You can also schedule a meeting directly from a **Customer** form. Go to the customer for whom you want to schedule a meeting and open the form view. In the list of actions at the right side of the screen, click *Schedule a Meeting*. If you stay in the Month view of the Calendar, you just have to click the day you want the meeting to be planned, let's say Thursday in two weeks. A meeting form will be displayed, with the name of the customer and the date prefilled.

Another way to enter a meeting request, is to directly use the meeting calendar from the menu *Sales → Meetings → Meetings*. You can use the monthly, weekly or daily views to plan a meeting by selecting the corresponding buttons. You can also click a day in the Navigator window to schedule a meeting.

In the **Meeting** window, enter the meeting data such as meeting summary, type, duration. In the weekly and daily views, you can also press the left mouse button in the calendar and slide the mouse along to create an event of several hours. OpenERP then opens an entry screen for a new meeting. You can add reminders (or `Alarms`) to your meetings and send invitations, either to persons from your own company, partner contacts or external people (just specify the email address directly in the invitation). You can send invitations before or after confirmation of a meeting. Either from the meeting itself or from the separate *Event Invitations* view in the menu *Sales → Configuration → Calendar → Event Invitations*, you can track and change the attendee statuses. If you cannot attend a meeting, you can delegate it to one of your colleagues.

**Alarms or Meeting Reminders**

Add your own alarms through *Sales → Configuration → Calendar → Alarms*. You might want to be warned one week in advance of the meeting, so all you have to do is create your own alarm. The screenshot below will show you how to do this.

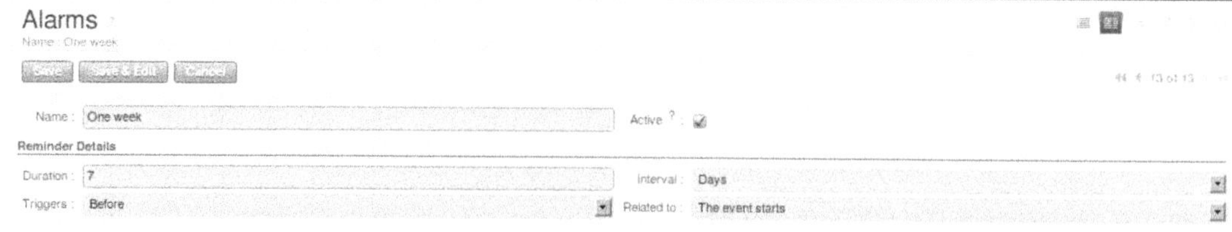


Figure 5.6: *Defining your Own Alarms*

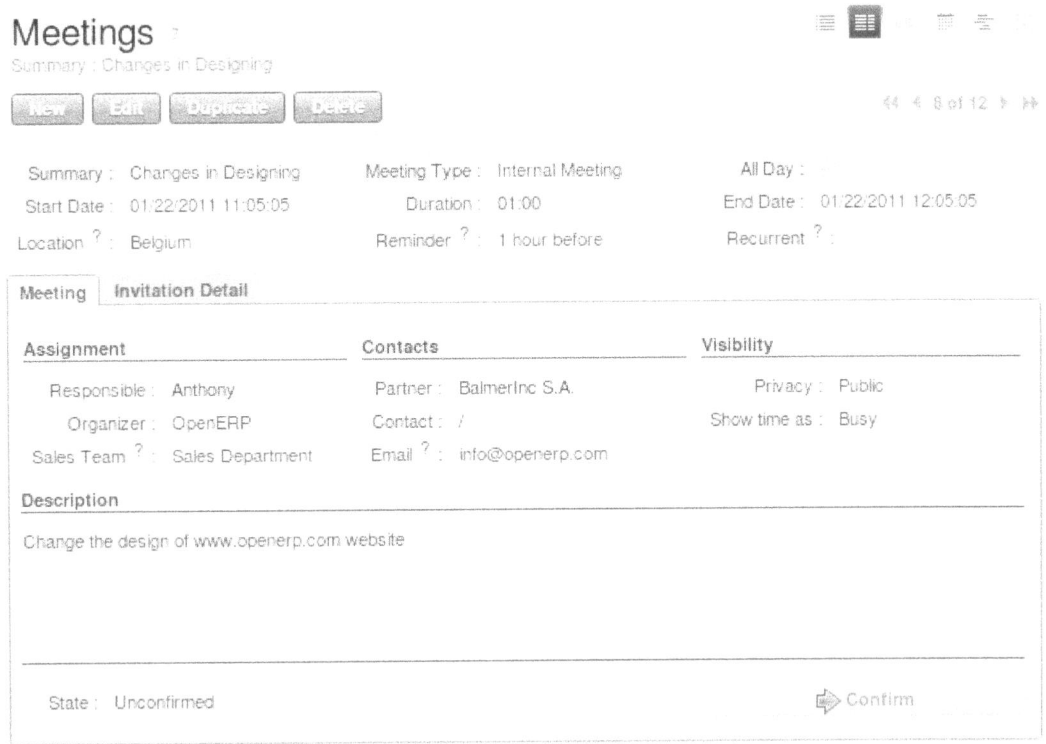


Figure 5.7: *Entering a New Meeting*

You may notice different colours and styles in the calendar. That is because OpenERP distinguishes between recurring events, multiple days events and events that only happen once. Multi-day events have a coloured background, whereas single events have a coloured font. Each event has a colour that represents the user who created the meeting. You can filter the different users by selecting them from the list at the right of the screen.

You can change the Calendar view for meetings and return to the list, form or gantt view by using the buttons at the top right. OpenERP's usual search tools and filters enable you to filter the events displayed in the calendar or, for example, to display the calendar for only some employees at a time.

**Related Partner**

When you hover your mouse cursor over a meeting in Calendar view, the related partner and the sales team will be displayed.

Of course, you can access this OpenERP calendar from your smartphone. For more information about this feature, please refer to chapter *Synchronizing your CRM with Mobile Devices* (page 67).

OpenERP also allows you to manage incoming (*inbound*) and outgoing (*outbound*) calls. Even from the **Phone Calls** list view, you can directly edit a call (change the status, convert it to an opportunity or schedule a meeting). For every call, you can enter notes about the outcome. While on the phone with

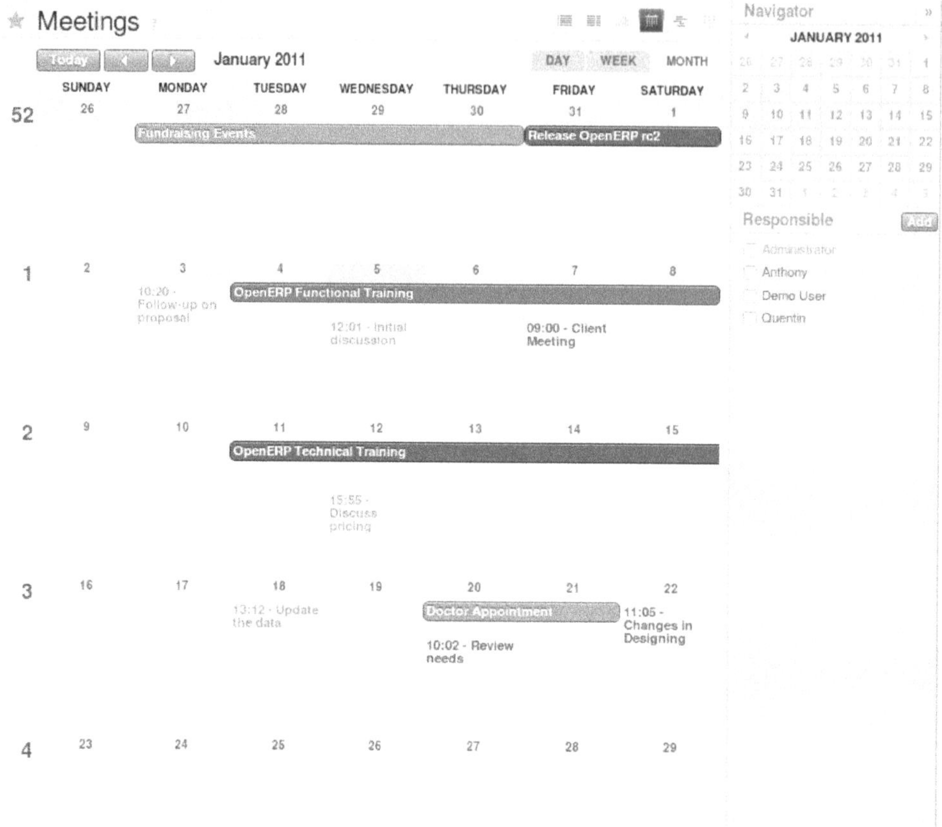


Figure 5.8: *Monthly Meeting Calendar*

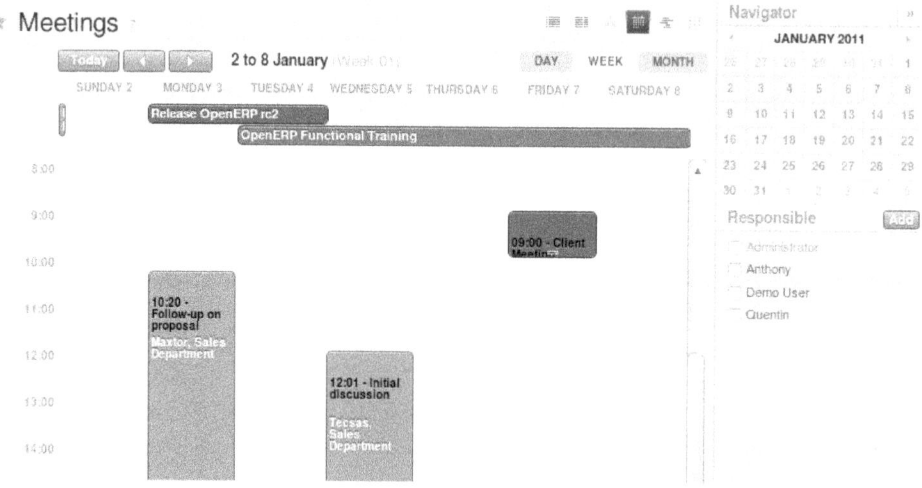


Figure 5.9: *Weekly Meeting Calendar*

your prospect or customer, you can directly schedule a meeting, schedule another call or convert your call to an opportunity. There is no need for you to scroll to several menus to do what you have to: plan an action as a result of your call.

Call management may be used for other needs than planning, such as:

- Entering customer calls so that you keep a record of the communication attached to a partner or a sales opportunity,
- Calling out to large lists of prospects,
- Scheduling recurring calls or next actions.

**Schedule a Phone Call directly**

Go to *Sales* → *Phone Calls* → *Inbound* to register incoming calls or *Outbound* to register outgoing calls.

The phone call will then be visible in the *History* tab of the **Partner** form to give you complete visibility of the events for a customer or supplier.

Of course, OpenERP also allows you to schedule a phone call directly from an **Opportunity** form through the related `Schedule/Log Call` button.

**Phone Calls in Meeting Calendar**

To have one calendar with both your meetings and your phone calls, you may choose to enter phone calls as a meeting, with a specific meeting type, *Phone Call*.

## 5.6 Scheduling Closing Dates

To keep track of the coming sales pipeline, you should enter the expected closing date for each opportunity. By doing this, from the **Opportunities** screen you can easily filter your pipeline by `Expected Closing` (button in Group by). This is a clear way to forecast the expected revenues. You can also use this filter to check whether the expected closing date has been set.

Simply by adding an expected closing date, the sales team can manage the sales process more efficiently and effectively.

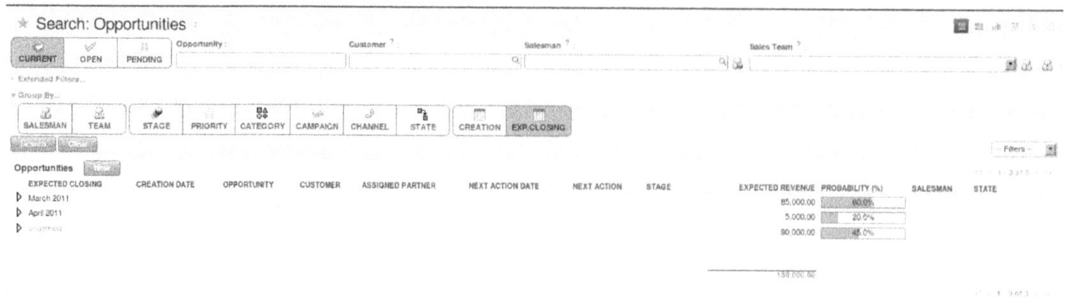


Figure 5.10: *Closing Dates*

# Connecting with your Email and Accessing from your Mobile Device 6

*OpenERP provides all the information you need to pursue your company's business opportunities effectively. But to stay productive with all the information you have to handle, it is essential that you can keep using your normal communication tools by interfacing them with OpenERP, and that you are not limited just to OpenERP's interface.*

Often your sales persons are already used to working with standard email clients to manage their business. OpenERP allows you to perfectly integrate their knowledge with the use of OpenERP.

OpenERP offers this flexibility to those who need to continue using their traditional email programs to maintain their efficiency: OpenERP can be connected to Outlook and Thunderbird. Your users can participate in many OpenERP-maintained processes without ever leaving their familiar environment, and can avoid double data entry, yet easily link information to OpenERP's database automatically.

With the Outlook and Thunderbird plug-ins, you can create and/or open contacts directly from your email client in OpenERP without effort. You can also link emails (with attachments) to OpenERP, to avoid information getting lost. Both plug-ins enable you for instance to create leads based on exchanges you have with the customer.

The email gateway functionality enables you to use Open ERP's CRM without necessarily using the OpenERP interface. Up-to-date leads can automatically be stored in OpenERP just by sending and receiving emails through a specific email address. You can even answer such mails from your own mailbox.

And of course, you can link the OpenERP meeting calendar to your mobile device.

## 6.1 Communication Tools

The *Fetchmail / Mailgateway* functionality lets you interface the CRM with incoming and outgoing emails. So you can receive mails in OpenERP and answer them directly from OpenERP. You can install it when you configure the CRM, through the *Reconfigure* wizard, *Fetch Emails*, or by installing the `fetchmail` module from the list of modules. Thanks to this feature, each email you receive on the specified email address may automatically create a lead, a contact or an other object in OpenERP, while keeping track of email attachments. This is an easy way to ensure that no crucial sales information gets lost.

You set the generic email address you want to use, such as sales@mycompany.com, and then you tell OpenERP that every incoming email for this address should automatically be created as a lead.

**Objects**

You can use this feature for any object in OpenERP, so for instance also to keep track of your helpdesk or job applications.

To use the email gateway, you should install the *Fetchmail* module. You might need a system administrator to carry out this work.

If you followed the steps in the previous chapters, you should have the *Fetchmail* module installed. If not, you can install the *Fetchmail* module from the Configuration Wizard (CRM Configuration Wizard, Synchronization, Fetch Emails), or from the modules list.

**Scheduled Action**

Click the `Fetch email` button to get the emails directly. OpenERP also automatically creates a **Scheduled Action** to fetch the mails every 5 minutes.

*Step 1*

You can configure your incoming mail account(s) from the *Sales → Configuration → Emails → Email Servers*.

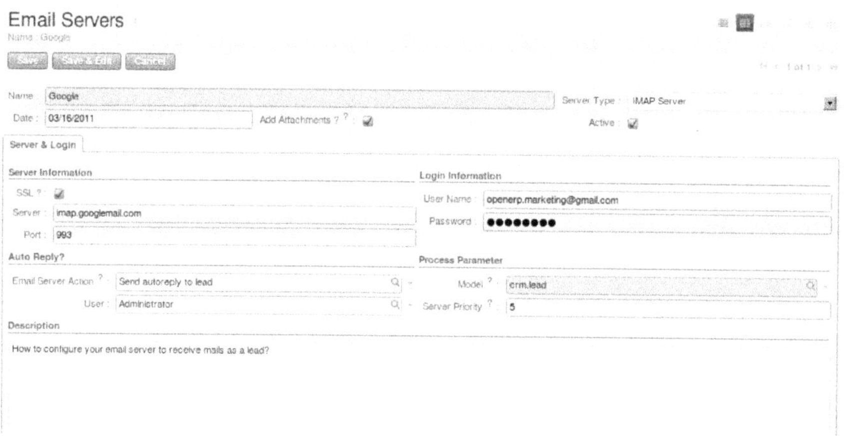


Figure 6.1: *How to Configure your Email Server for Incoming Mails?*

Go to *Tools → Configuration → Email Template → Email Accounts* to define the email smtp settings.

In the `Description` field, type the visible name you would like to use for the account.

In `Server`, type the mail server, i.e. smtp.googlemail.com.

Type the SMTP port (e.g. 587), configure the other settings according to the specifications of your server.

Add the User Information, such as email address for which the mails will enter OpenERP, i.e. support@mycompany.com, the user name and the password. Configure the other settings to your needs.

Save and click the `Test Outgoing Connection` button to check whether the settings are correct.

When everything is correctly configured, *Approve* the account. OpenERP will automatically create a Scheduler for the mails. You can also send/receive mails manually by clicking the `Send/Receive` button.

*Step 2*

You can configure your outgoing mail account(s) from the *Tools → Configuration → Email Template → Email Accounts*.

Figure 6.2: *How to Configure your Email Server for Outgoing Mails?*

Go to Sales > Configuration > Emails > Email Servers to define the email server settings.

Assign a `Name` and select the `Server Type`, i.e. IMAP Server.

Click `Add Attachments` if you want to include attachments for the mails received / sent.

Enter the Server Information, check SSL if necessary, i.e. imap.googlemail.com and the Login Information.

You can also choose to send an automatic reply on receipt of the mail. You can configure the mail here from the `Email Server Action` field.

Assign the `Model` to use when a new email arrives, i.e. choose Lead (crm.leads) if you want every new email that arrives to be created as a lead.

Click *Confirm* to confirm the account settings.

**Server Configuration**

You will also have your administrator to configure your server settings to allow for an email gateway. This will not be explained in this book.

## 6.2 Managing your CRM from Microsoft Outlook

The Microsoft Outlook plug-in enables you to carry out a series of OpenERP operations quickly and directly from the Outlook email client:

- create a contact or partner from an email,
- open a partner from an email,
- save an email and its attachments in OpenERP from your mailbox,
- send any attachment to an OpenERP document (such as opportunities, customers).

Thanks to the plug-in, you can effortlessly link emails and attachments to the corresponding opportunity in OpenERP, or link an attached product folder to a customer, for instance.

**Outlook Versions**

The Microsoft Outlook plug-in works with Microsoft Outlook 2003 and 2007, but not with Outlook Express.

In this chapter, only the actual possibilities of the plug-in will be discussed. For more information about how to install and configure the Outlook plug-in, please refer to the chapter *outlook*.

From the Outlook toolbar, have a look at the *Tools* menu.

The *Push* option allows you to archive emails to OpenERP, either to new document types or to existing ones (such as Leads). It also allows you to create a new contact.

The *Partner* option allows you to open the Partner in OpenERP according to the email (i.e. contact email address) selected.

With *Document*, you can open the document (i.e. a customer, an opportunity) concerned in OpenERP. Make sure your web server is running to use this functionality.

- Link an email to an existing document in OpenERP

To archive an email in OpenERP from Outlook, select the email and click the *Push* button. Alternatively you can open the menu *Tools* → *Push*: the `Push to OpenERP` screen will open.

In the `Link to an Existing Document` section, check *Partner*. Then select the customer you want to attach the selected mail to. The plug-in also allows you to select several customers at once, simply by selecting a customer and pressing the `ctrl` button while selecting the next one.

Suppose you decide to no longer link the selected email to a customer, but instead to an opportunity. Then you have to click the `Search` button to refresh the *Documents* list to display your opportunities.

From the list of available documents, you can select any document type you defined in the `Document Settings` section.

- Create a New Document

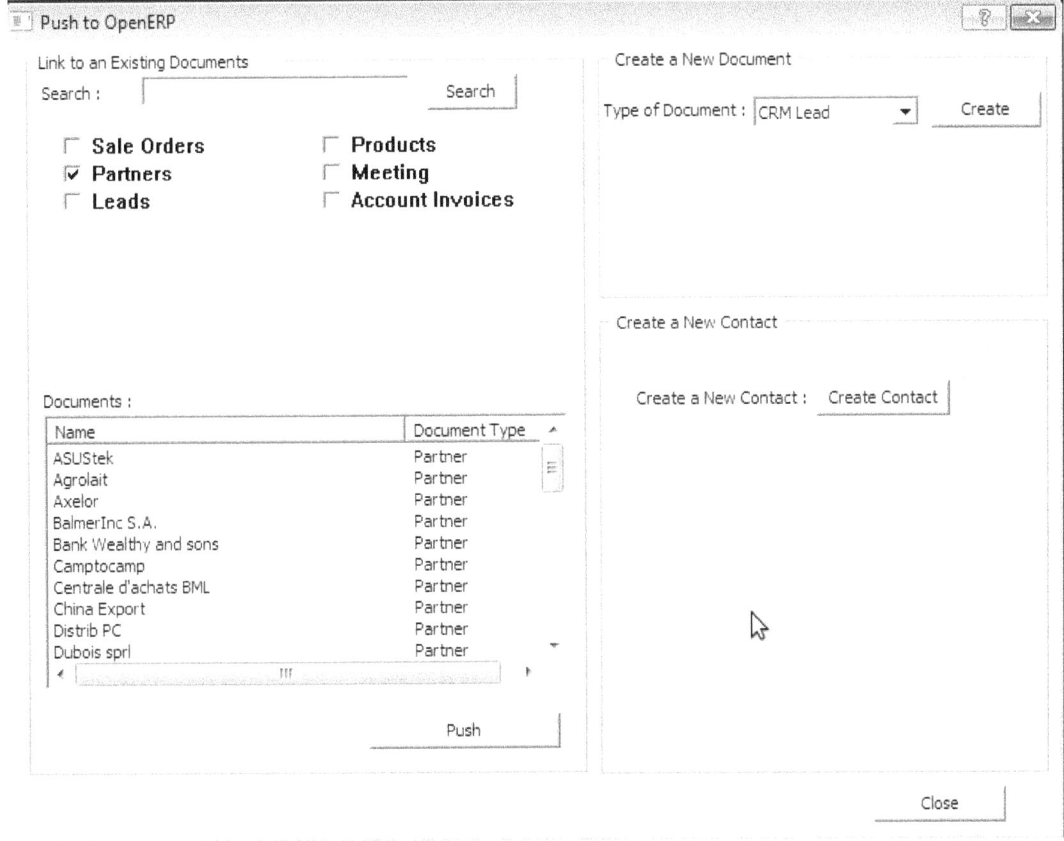


Figure 6.3: *How to Access OpenERP from Outlook?*

This feature can be used to create any of the configured document types in the `Document Settings` tab. Suppose you would like to create a new lead from an email. In the `Create a New Document` section, select `CRM Lead`, then click the `Create` button. A new lead will be created in OpenERP from the selected email.

- Create a New Contact / Partner

If the partner or contact from your email does not exist in OpenERP yet, the Outlook plug-in allows you to create one on the fly simply by using the information contained in the email.

Select the email from which you want to create a new contact, then click the `Push` button. In the `Create a New Contact` section, click the `New Contact` button. This option offers two possibilities: either you just create a contact (address), or you create a partner with the contact linked to it.

- When you just want to create a new contact, complete the address data in the dialog box and click the `Save` button. The contact will then be created in OpenERP.
- When you also want to create a new partner, complete the contact data. Then click the `Create`

`Partner` button, add the partner's name and click the `Save` button.

- You can also add a new contact to an existing partner. Click the `Search` button next to the Partner field and select the corresponding partner from the list. Then complete the contact data and click the `Save` button.

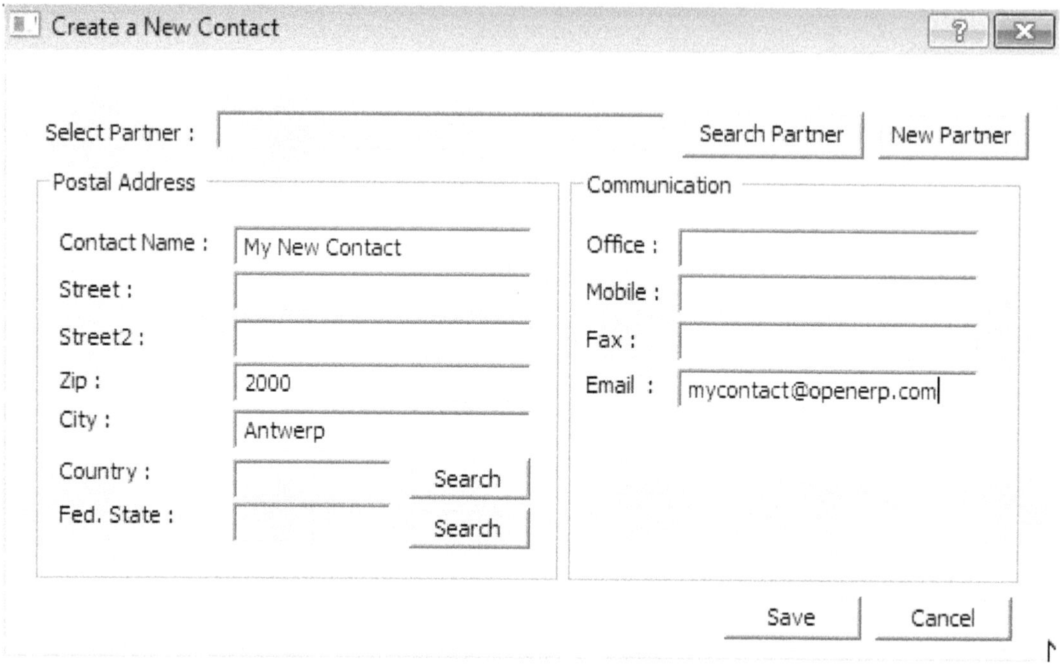

Figure 6.4: *Creating a Contact on the Fly from Outlook*

- Open the Document created in OpenERP

From your mailbox, simply by clicking an email, you can directly access the corresponding data in OpenERP. Go to the menu *Tools* → *Document* which will open the corresponding document (e.g. a lead) in OpenERP, directly from the email you selected.

**Knowledge Management**

The Outlook plug-in is compatible with OpenERP's Knowledge (i.e. Document) Management. If you install the Knowledge application you will be able to:

- search through the content of your company's documents (those that have the type .doc, .pdf, .sxw and .odt) and also in archived emails,
- have a shared file system that is connected to various OpenERP documents to share information and access it with your favorite browser,
- organize and structure your documents (such as projects, partners and users) in OpenERP's system.

- Step 1: Install the Outlook plugin in OpenERP

Use the OpenERP Configuration Wizard and install the `Customer Relationship Management` application. In the *CRM Application Configuration* dialog under Plug-In, select *MS-Outlook*. Then the *Outlook Plug-In* wizard appears. Next to the `Outlook Plug-in` field, click the `Save As` button to save the plugin to your desktop (or any other location on your computer).

You can also download the installation manual by clicking the green arrow next to `Installation Manual`.

Another way to use the Outlook plugin, is by installing the OpenERP module `outlook`. When you install this module, the same Configuration Wizard as explained before will be displayed. Follow the same instructions.

- Step 2: Prerequisites (for more details, please refer to the online documentation)

  1. Install Python 2.6+
  2. Python for Windows extensions - PyWin32, this module for python must be installed for the appropriate version of Python.
  3. Specify the python folder in the system path (typically with this installer C:Python26)

  *How to set the path in Windows XP* For Windows XP: http://www.computerhope.com/issues/ch000549.htm

  *How to set the path in Windows 7* To change the system environment variables, follow the steps below.

  - From the Windows button, select `Control Panel`, then click `System`.
  - Click `Remote Settings` to open the System Properties window.
  - In the System Properties window, click the Advanced tab.
  - In the Advanced section, click the `Environment Variables` button.

- Finally, in the Environment Variables window (as shown below) under System Variables, highlight the Path directory, click Edit and add ;C:Python26.

4. If you are using MS Outlook 2007 then you are required to install "Microsoft Exchange Server MAPI Client and Collaboration Data Objects 1.2.1 (CDO 1.21)" Double-click Exchange CDO to install it.

5. If you are using MS Outlook 2003, be sure to install the built-in CDO component.

- Step 3: Install the OpenERP extension in Outlook.

  1. Double-click the file ''OpenERP-Outlook-addin.exe''that you saved on your desktop. Confirm the default settings.
  2. Double-click the file ''Register plugin''in the OpenERP Outlook Addin folder (typically in C:Program Files).
  3. Start Outlook.

When you have executed Installation Step 1, Step 2 and Step 3, the first thing to do is connect Outlook to OpenERP. A little configuration needs to be done.

**Toolbars**

If you want the OpenERP connection to be shown as a separate toolbar, go to the menu *View → Toolbars*. Select `OpenERP`.

- Go to the menu *Tools* and select *Configuration*. If this raises an error, make sure to check the access rights to that particular folder.

A configuration window appears enabling you to enter configuration data about your OpenERP server.

When your connection has succeeded, you would typically want to configure Outlook to fit your needs.

To define extra document types, go to the *Document Settings* tab. This is the place where you can add objects from OpenERP that you wish to link mails to. The default installation comes with a number of predefined documents, such as Partners, Leads and Sales Orders.

Here is an example of how to configure extra document types. Suppose you would like to link mails to a meeting:

1. In the *Title*, type `Meeting`,
2. In the *Document*, type the object from OpenERP, in this example `crm.meeting`,
3. In the *Image*, select an icon you would like to use,
4. Click the *Add* button to actually create the document type.

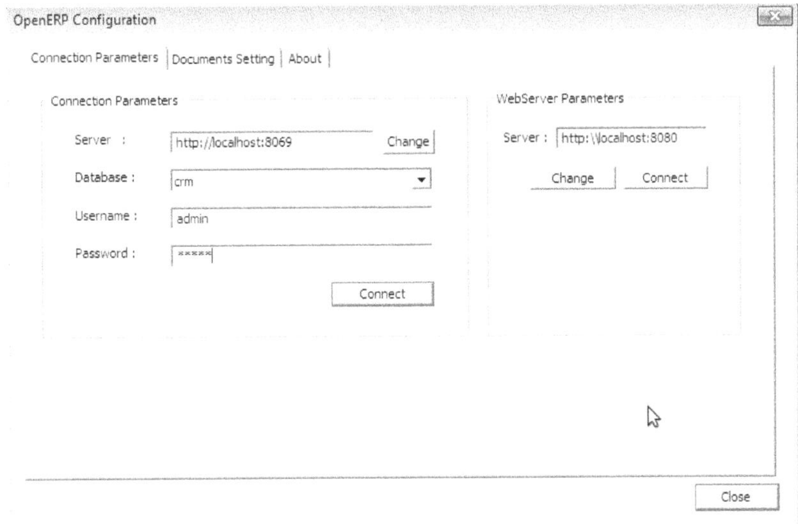


Figure 6.5: *How to Connect to the Server*

1. On the `Configuration Settings` tab, under *Connection Parameters* click the *Change* button and type your server settings and XML-RPC port, e.g. `http://127.0.0.1:8069`,
2. Select the database you want to connect to, and type the user and the password required to log in to the database,
3. Click the *Connect* button,
4. On the `Configuration Settings` tab, under *Webserver Parameters* click the *Change* button and type your web server settings, e.g. `http://localhost:8080`,
5. Click the *Open* button to test the connection.

**A Word about Objects**

To find the object you need in OpenERP, go to the menu *Administration → Customization → Database Structure → Objects*. OpenERP will only show objects for which the corresponding Business Applications / Modules have been installed. You can only add objects to Outlook that are available in the selected database.

## 6.3 Managing your CRM from Mozilla Thunderbird

With the Mozilla Thunderbird plug-in you can carry out a series of OpenERP operations directly from Thunderbird, such as:

- create a contact or partner from an email,
- open a partner from an email,

- save an email and its attachments in OpenERP,
- send any attachment to an OpenERP document (such as opportunities, customers).

Thanks to the plug-in, you can effortlessly link emails and attachments to the corresponding opportunity in OpenERP, or link an attached product folder to a customer, for instance.

In this chapter, only the actual possibilities of the plug-in will be discussed. For more information about how to install and configure the Thunderbird plug-in, please refer to the chapter *thunderbird*.

From the Thunderbird toolbar, have a look at the *OpenERP* menu.

The *Push* option allows you to archive emails to OpenERP, either to new document types or to existing ones. It also allows you to create a new contact.

The *Partner* allows you to open the Partner in OpenERP according to the email (i.e. contact email address) selected.

With *Document*, you can open the document (i.e. a customer, an opportunity) concerned in OpenERP. Make sure your web server is running to use this functionality. You have to open the mail to use this feature.

- Link an email to an existing document in OpenERP

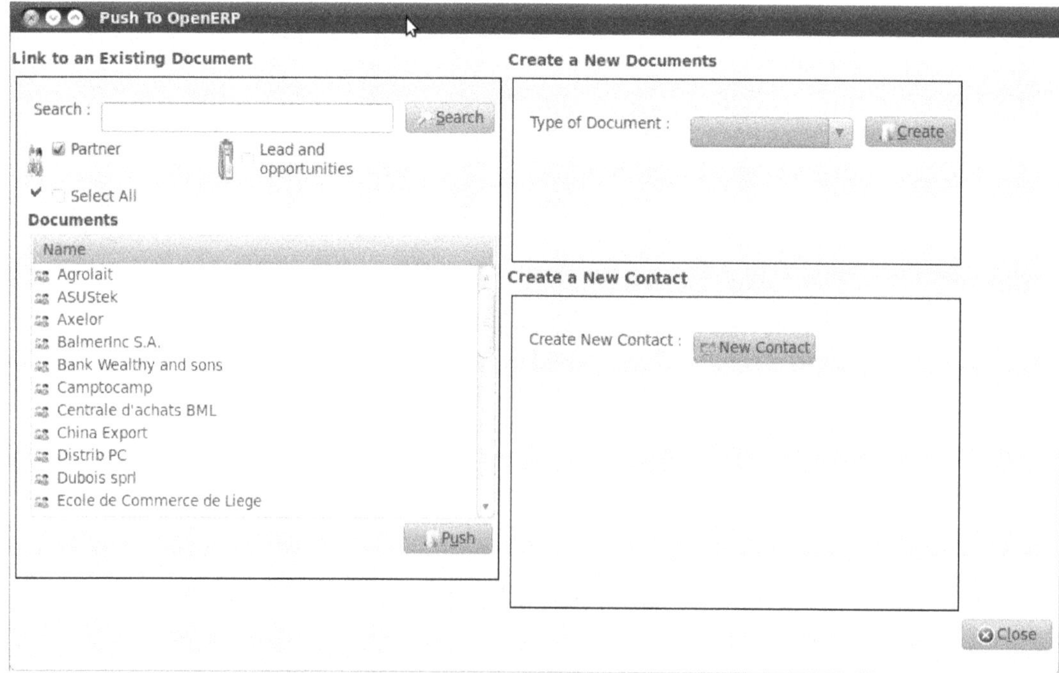


Figure 6.6: *How to Access OpenERP from Thunderbird?*

To archive an email in OpenERP from Thunderbird, select the email and click the *Push* button. Alternatively you can open the menu *OpenERP* → *Push*: the `Push to OpenERP` screen will open.

In the `Link to an Existing Document` section, check *Partner*. Then select the customer you want to attach the selected mail to. The plug-in also allows you to select several customers at once, simply by selecting a customer and pressing the `ctrl` button while selecting the next one.

Suppose you decide to no longer link the selected email to a customer, but instead to an opportunity. Then you have to click the `Search` button to refresh the *Documents* list to display your opportunities.

From the list of available documents, you can select any document type you defined in the `Document Settings` section.

- Create a New Document

This feature can be used to create any of the configured document types in the `Document Settings` tab. Suppose you would like to create a new lead from an email. In the `Create a New Document` section, select `CRM Lead`, then click the `Create` button. A new lead will be created in OpenERP from the selected email.

- Create a New Contact / Partner

If the partner or contact from your email does not exist in OpenERP yet, the Thunderbird plug-in allows you to create one on the fly simply by using the information contained in the email.

Select the email from which you want to create a new contact, then click the `Push` button. In the `Create a New Contact` section, click the `New Contact` button. This option offers two possibilities: either you just create a contact (address), or you create a partner with the contact linked to it.

- When you just want to create a new contact, complete the address data in the dialog box and click the `Save` button. The contact will then be created in OpenERP.
- When you also want to create a new partner, complete the contact data. Then click the `Create Partner` button, add the partner's name and click the `Save` button.
- You can also add a new contact to an existing partner. Click the `Search` button next to the Partner field and select the corresponding partner from the list. Then complete the contact data and click the `Save` button.

- Open the Document created in OpenERP

From your mailbox, simply by clicking an email, you can directly access the corresponding data in OpenERP. Go to the menu *Tools* → *Document* which will open the corresponding document (e.g. a lead) in OpenERP, directly from the email you selected.

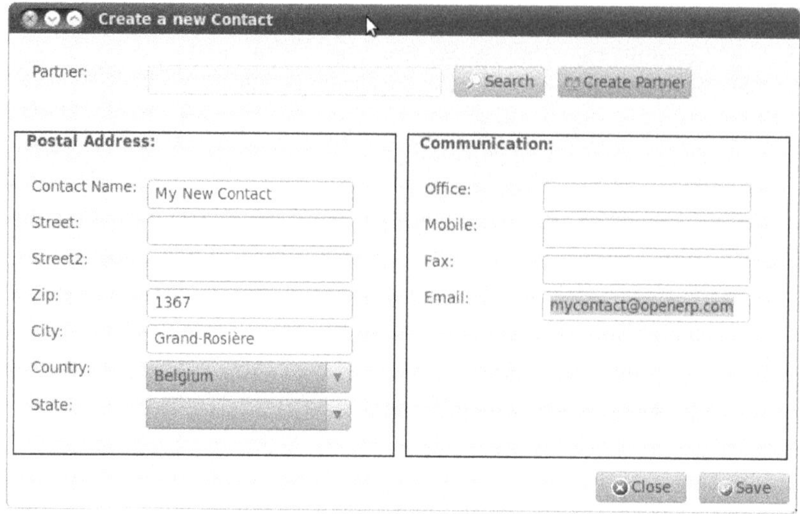


Figure 6.7: *Creating a Contact on the Fly from Thunderbird*

**Knowledge Management**

The Thunderbird plug-in is compatible with OpenERP's Knowledge (i.e. Document) Management. If you install the Knowledge application you will be able to:

- search through the content of your company's documents (those that have the type .doc, .pdf, .sxw and .odt) and also in archived emails,
- have a shared file system that is connected to various OpenERP documents to share information and access it with your favorite browser,
- organize and structure your documents (such as projects, partners and users) in OpenERP's system.

- Step 1: Install the Thunderbird plugin in OpenERP

Use the OpenERP Configuration Wizard and install the `Customer Relationship Management` application. In the *CRM Application Configuration* dialog under Plug-In, select *Thunderbird*. Then the *Thunderbird Plug-In* wizard appears. Next to the `Thunderbird Plug-in` field, click the `Save As` button to save the plugin to your desktop (or any other location on your computer).

You can also download the installation manual by clicking the orange arrow next to `Installation Manual`.

Another way to use the Thunderbird plugin, is by installing the OpenERP module `thunderbird`. When you install this module, the same Configuration Wizard as explained before will be displayed. Follow the same instructions.

- Step 2: Install the OpenERP extension in Thunderbird.

To do that, use the file ''openerp_plugin.xpi''that you saved on your desktop.

Then proceed as follows:

1. From Thunderbird, open the menu *Tools → Add-ons*.
2. Click Extensions, then click the *Install* button.
3. Go to your desktop and select the file `openerp_plugin.xpi`. Click Open.
4. Click *Install Now* then restart Thunderbird.

Once the extension has been installed, a new `OpenERP` menu item is added to your Thunderbird menubar.

**Thunderbird Version**

The OpenERP plugin for Thunderbird works as from Thunderbird version 2.0.

So check your Thunderbird version before installing, and download the latest version that you need from the following address: http://www.mozilla.org/products/thunderbird/

When you have executed Installation Step 1 and Step 2, the first thing to do is connect Thunderbird to OpenERP. A little configuration needs to be done.

**Before starting the configuration, make sure your GTK server and web server are running (XML-RPC should be allowed).**

Go to the `OpenERP` menubar and select ' Configuration'.

A configuration window appears enabling you to enter configuration data about your OpenERP server.

When your connection has succeeded, you would typically want to configure Thunderbird to fit your needs.

To define extra document types, go to the *Document Settings* tab. This is the place where you can add objects from OpenERP that you wish to link mails to. The default installation comes with a number of predefined documents, such as Partners, Leads and Sales Orders.

Here is an example of how to configure extra document types. Suppose you would like to link mails to a purchase order.

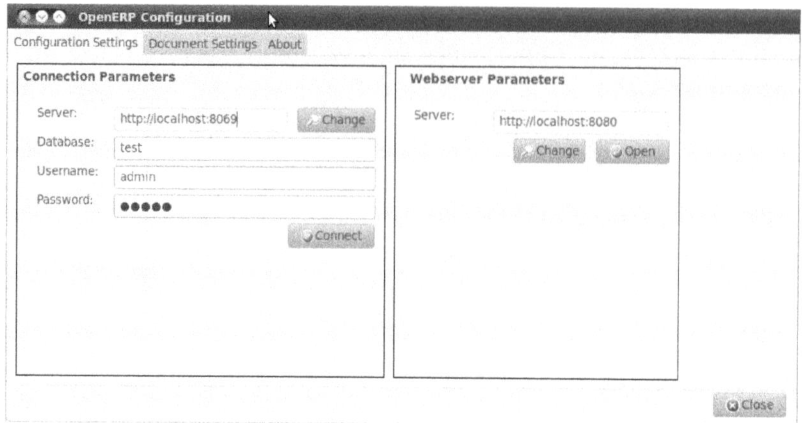


Figure 6.8: *How to Connect to the Server*

1. On the `Configuration Settings` tab, under *Connection Parameters* click the *Change* button and type your server settings and XML-RPC port, e.g. `http://127.0.0.1:8069`,
2. Select the database you want to connect to, and type the user and the password required to log in to the database,
3. Click the *Connect* button,
4. On the `Configuration Settings` tab, under *Webserver Parameters* click the *Change* button and type your web server settings, e.g. `http://localhost:8080`,
5. Click the *Open* button to test the connection.

1. In the *Title*, type `Purchase Order`,
2. In the *Document*, type the object from OpenERP, in this example `purchase.order`,
3. In the *Image*, select an icon you would like to use,
4. Click the *Add* button to actually create the document type.

**A Word about Objects**

To find the object you need in OpenERP, go to the menu *Administration* → *Customization* → *Database Structure* → *Objects*. OpenERP will only show objects for which the corresponding Business Applications / Modules have been installed. You can only add objects to Thunderbird that are available in the selected database.

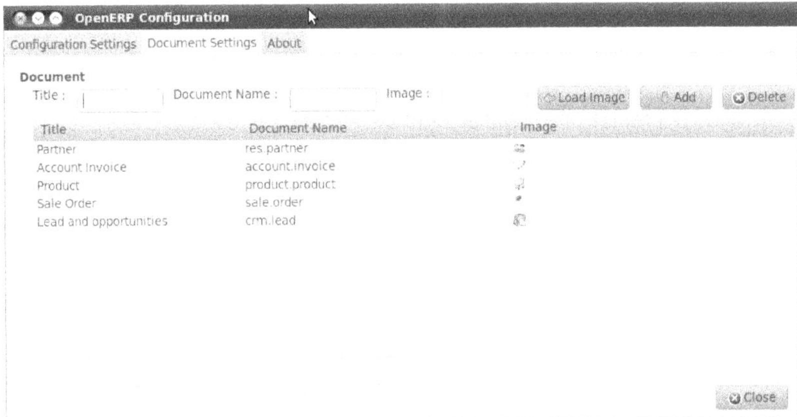


Figure 6.9: *How to Add Extra OpenERP Document Types to Thunderbird?*

## 6.4 Synchronizing your CRM with Mobile Devices

Synchronize your OpenERP calendars with your mobile device and know which meeting to go to from wherever you are!

Make your OpenERP even more efficient and let your sales synchronize their meetings with their mobile devices. Anywhere your sales people are, they can easily check their planning and confirm new meetings with customers on the spot.

You can synchronize your calendars with iPhone and Android phones, and also with tools such as Evolution and Sunbird/Lightning.

**Installation and Configuration**

Please note that setting this up requires some technical knowledge, and probably the assistance of IT staff.

### 6.4.1 OpenERP Server and SSL Setup

Some modules need to be installed on the OpenERP server (or may already be installed). These are:

- `caldav`: Required, has the reference setup and the necessary underlying code. Will also cause document & document_webdav to be installed.
- `crm_caldav`: Optional, will export the CRM Meetings as a calendar.
- `project_caldav`: Optional, will export project tasks as a calendar.
- `http_well_known`: Optional, experimental. Will ease bootstrapping, but only when a DNS srv record is also used.

When you install the above module(s), a ready-to-go reference setup of the folders is provided. The OpenERP administrator can add more calendars and (re)structure if needed.

It is highly advisable that you also set up SSL to work for the OpenERP server. HTTPS is a server-wide feature in OpenERP, which means a certificate will be set at the openerp-server.conf which will be the same for XML-RPC, HTTP, WebDAV and CalDAV. The iPhone also supports secure connections with SSL, although it does not expect a self-signed certificate (or one that is not verified by one of the "big" certificate authorities).

## 6.4.2 Calendars on iPhone

To set up the calendars, proceed as follows:

1. Click `Settings` and go to the `Mail, Contacts, Calendars` page.
2. Go to `Add account...`
3. Click `Other`.
4. From the `Calendars` group, select `Add CalDAV Account`.
5. Enter the host name (e.g. if the URL is http://openerp.com:8069/webdav/db_1/calendars/, openerp.com is the host).

> **Synchronize this Calendar**
>
> Go to *Sales* → *Meetings* → *Synchronize this Calendar* and select `Iphone`. Then the Caldav server will be shown.

6. In `Username` and `Password`, type your OpenERP login and password.
7. As a description, you can either leave the server's name or something like "OpenERP calendars".
8. If you are not using a SSL server, you will get an error, do not worry and push "Continue"
9. Then click "Advanced Settings" to specify the correct ports and paths.
10. Specify the port for the OpenERP server: 8071 for SSL, 8069 without SSL.
11. Set the `Account URL` to the right path of the OpenERP webdav: the URL given by the wizard (e.g. http://my.server.ip:8069/webdav/dbname/calendars/ )
12. Click `Done`. The phone will connect to the OpenERP server and verify whether the account can be used.
13. Go to the main menu of the iPhone and open the Calendar application. Your OpenERP calendars will be visible inside the selection of the "Calendars" button. Note that when creating a new calendar entry, you will have to specify which calendar it should be saved to.

If you need *SSL* (and your certificate is not a verified one), you will first need to let the iPhone trust the certificate. Follow these steps:

1. Open Safari and enter the HTTPS location of the OpenERP server: https://my.server.ip:8071/ (assuming you have the server at "my.server.ip" and the HTTPS port is the default 8071)
2. Safari will try to connect and issue a warning about the certificate used. Inspect the certificate and click "Accept" so that iPhone now trusts it.

## 6.4.3 Calendars on Android

### Prerequisites

There is no built-in way to synchronize calendars with CalDAV. So you need to install a third party software: Calendar (CalDav) Sync BETA from Hypermatix Software (for now, it is the only one).

### How to Configure?

1. Open the `Calendar Sync` application. You get an interface with 2 tabs.
2. On the *Connection* tab, in CalDAV Calendar URL, type a URL such as http://my.server.ip:8069/webdav/dbname/calendars/users/demo/c/Meetings.

**Synchronize this Calendar**

Go to *Sales* → *Meetings* → *Synchronize this Calendar* and select `Android`. Then the Caldav server link will be shown. Make sure to use the correct XML-RPC port, it may differ from 8069.

3. Type your OpenERP username and password.
4. If your server does not use SSL, you will get a warning. Answer `Yes`.
5. Then you can synchronize manually or customize the settings (*Sync* tab) to synchronize every X minutes.

## 6.4.4 Calendars in Evolution

1. Go to Calendar View.
2. *File* → *New* → *Calendar*.
3. Enter the data in the form:
   - Type : CalDav
   - Name : Whatever you want (e.g. Meeting)
   - URL : http://HOST:PORT/webdav/DB_NAME/calendars/users/USER/c/Meetings (e.g. http://localhost:8069/webdav/db_1/calendars/users/demo/c/Meetings) the one given on top of this window

- Uncheck "User SSL"
- Username : Your username (e.g. Demo)
- Refresh : every time you want Evolution to synchronize the data with the server

**Synchronize this Calendar**

Go to *Sales* → *Meetings* → *Synchronize this Calendar* and select `Evolution`. Then the Caldav server will be shown.

4. Click OK and enter your OpenERP password.
5. A new calendar with the name you entered should appear on the left side.

### 6.4.5 Calendars in Sunbird/Lightning

#### Prerequisites

If you are using Thunderbird, first install the Lightning module http://www.mozilla.org/projects/calendar/lightning/

#### Configuration

1. Go to Calendar View.
2. *File* → *New Calendar*.
3. Choose `On the Network`.
4. As a format, select CalDav and as a location type the URL (e.g. http://host.com:8069/webdav/db/calendars/users/demo/c/Meetings).

**Synchronize this Calendar**

Go to *Sales* → *Meetings* → *Synchronize this Calendar* and select `Sunbird/Lightning`. Then the Caldav server will be shown.

5. Choose a name and a colour for the Calendar, and we advice you to uncheck "alarm".
6. Enter your OpenERP login and password (to give the password only once, check the box `Use Password Manager to remember this password`).
7. Then click Finish; your meetings should now appear in your Calendar view.

# Managing your Indirect Sales 7

OpenERP will help you to manage your Channel Partners. You can geolocalize your opportunities by going to *Administration → Modules → Modules* and then typing `crm_partner_assign` in the `Name` field. Check the module and click the button at the end of the line (after the `State` field) to plan the module for installation. Notice that the `State` will change to 'To be installed'. In the Actions at the right, click *Apply Scheduled Upgrades*. The module will be installed and the menus *Sales → Configuration → Leads & Opportunities → Partner Grade* and *Sales → Reporting → Opportunity Assignment Analysis* will be added.

**CRM Configuration Wizard**

When you click *Apply Scheduled Upgrades*, the Configuration Wizard will be displayed. You can cancel it if you need no other CRM modules to be installed.

## 7.1 Forwarding Opportunities to Channel Partners

You can use geolocalization to assign and forward opportunities to channel partners.

Through *Sales → Configuration → Leads & Opportunities → Partner Grade*, you can create partner grades to classify your partners, such as Gold Partner, Silver Partner, Ready Partner. These grades will be used to determine who gets assigned which kind of opportunities.

Assign the grades to the partners on the *Geo Localization* tab of the Customer form. Also assign a *Weight* to determine the probability of assigning opportunities to a partner. The weight might for instance be the amount that the partner pays for his channel partner contract.

How can you tell OpenERP to geolocalize an opportunity?

Either you convert a promising lead to an opportunity, or you go directly to the opportunity you wish to assign to the channel partner. Go to the *Assignation* tab of the **Opportunities** form, and click the *Geo Assign* button. The location of the partner in the opportunity will be matched with the geolatitude and the weight of the channel partners. The most appropriate channel partner will be assigned.

**GPS**

You can also use the geolocalization without using the GPS coordinates.

Now you can decide whether this is the correct channel partner for this opportunity. If you feel that another channel partner would be better to follow up this opportunity because he , you can change the assigned channel partner.

To automatically inform the channel partner of the new opportunity, proceed as follows.

Click the `Forward` button to automatically send an email to the assigned partner with all the details of the opportunity and the prospect. When forwarding an opportunity to a partner, you can select which information you want to send: Latest email, Whole Story or Case Information. You can add a cc and add attachments to the mail. You can decide to send the mail to the partner (any contact person you want), to an OpenERP user or to an email address you specify.

To allow your salespeople to keep a view on forwarded opportunities, the assigned opportunity will be displayed for the selected channel partner on the *Geo Localization* tab of the **Customer** form.

Use the **Opportunity Assignment Analysis** for your reporting.

**Google Maps**

Use the geolocalization together with the google_map module. This adds a Map button to your **Partner** form. Click this button to open a browser with the partner's location displayed in Google Maps.

## 7.2 Geolocalization of a Partner

To determine the geographic location of your partners, you do not have to enter the GPS coordinates yourself. OpenERP can do this for you. All you have to do is click the `Geo Localize` button in the **Customer** form. The GPS coordinates will now be filled according to the address of the partner.

In the partner form, the *Geo Localization* tab gives you the information you need.

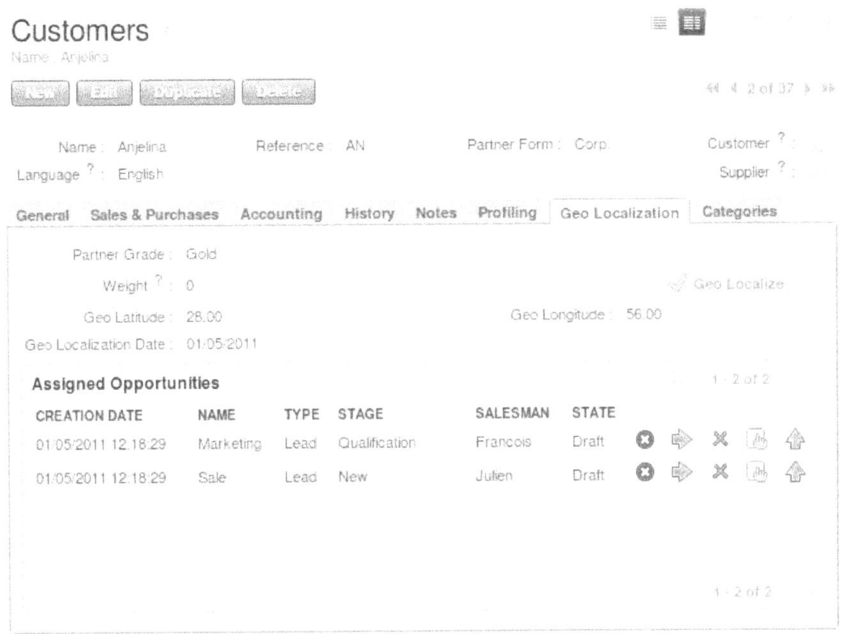


Figure 7.1: *Geolocalizing a Partner*

# Keeping Track of your Communications 8

## 8.1 Tracking your Customer's History

Information related to leads & opportunities, meetings, phone calls, marketing campaigns and emails will be tracked in OpenERP. The activities are automatically reported in the partner form of the associated customer. To have a complete overview of the activities for a customer, all you have to do is open the **Customer** form and click the *History* tab. As you will notice in the screenshot below, this is not merely a report. From this tab, you can also plan new activities for the customer or change existing activities!

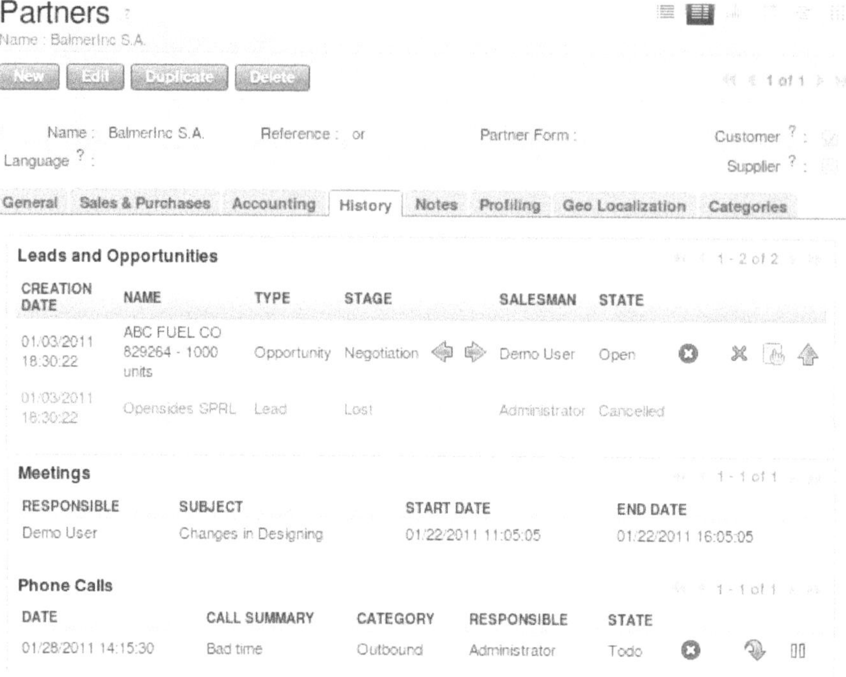


Figure 8.1: *History of Activities in a Customer Form*

## 8.2 Tracking Sales Orders

After intensive opportunity qualification, your customer asks you to make a quotation. You can easily do this from the corresponding opportunity! Just click the `Convert to Quote` button and OpenERP will create a sales quotation ready for you to be edited. A sales quotation is an unconfirmed sales order. On the quotation, the Source document it was created from (in this case the opportunity) is displayed, to allow you to keep track of which opportunity is linked to which sales quotation / order.

To review the quotation later, you can access it from the *Sales* → *Sales* → *Sales Orders* menu. On the *Extra Info* tab of the sales quotation, you can find the reference to the related sales quotation / order that has been created from the opportunity concerned.

For more information about sales orders, please refer to the chapter *Closing your Deals: from Quotation to Sales Order* (page 97).

## 8.3 Storing Attached Documents

For any object in OpenERP, for instance a lead, opportunity, customer, you can attach external documents. Suppose you send a product folder to one of your customers, and to make sure you know exactly which version of the document he received, you can keep it as an attachment in OpenERP.

To attach whatever type of document to the customer, you just have to go to the *Sales* → *Address Book*

→ *Customers* menu.

Open the Customer form of the selected partner, and click the *Add* button in the Action bar, just below *Attachments*. Then click the *Browse...* button and navigate to the location where the product folder is stored, just like you would do in your file explorer. Click the product folder, and then confirm.

The product folder is now stored in OpenERP as an attachment for the customer. You can open it by clicking the document in Attachments.

OpenERP allows you to add as many attachments as needed. Combined with the *Knowledge* application, OpenERP will index documents of the type .doc, .pdf, .sxw and .odt, so that you can effortlessly search through their content.

**File Storage**

If you do not install the Document Management system (*Knowledge* application) then the attachments in OpenERP are stored directly in the database. Once the document management system has been installed, the contents of the files are no longer stored in the database, but on the OpenERP server file system.

You can then read and add attachments to OpenERP quite independently of the OpenERP interface or the FTP server using simple drag and drop.

For more information about the Knowledge and Document Management System, please refer to the online documentation.

# Part III

# Driving your Marketing Campaigns

# Lead Automation with Marketing Campaigns

# 9

OpenERP offers a set of modules allowing you to easily create and track your Marketing Campaigns. With the **Marketing** application, you define your direct marketing campaigns, allowing you to automate your lead communication. You can install the module through the Reconfigure wizard, then select Marketing.

Campaigns can be displayed in List or Diagram view. The Diagram view allows you to clearly see the marketing actions (represented by a node) and the applied conditions (represented by an arrow).

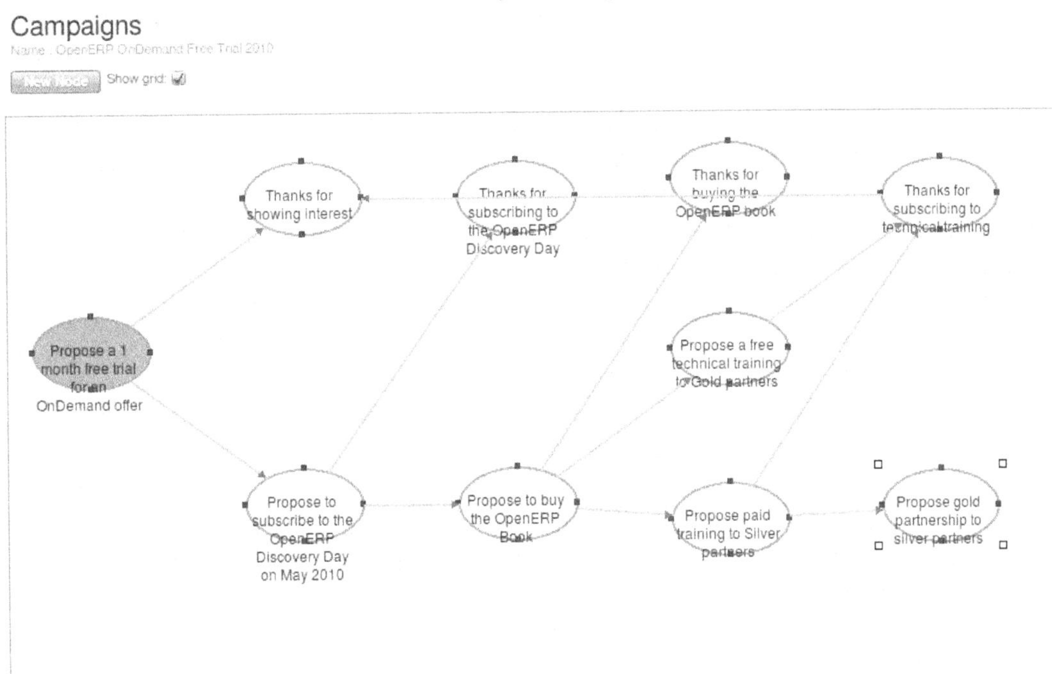


Figure 9.1: *Diagram View of a Campaign*

A marketing campaign is an event or an activity that will help you manage and reach your partners with specific messages. A campaign can have many activities that will be triggered from a specific situation, for instance a response from a contact to an email you sent. The result of such a response (action) could be the sending of an email, for which a template has previously been created in OpenERP.

To use the email functionality, you have to configure your email account. This is explained in the chapter *Communication Tools* (page 53).

## 9.1 Example of a Complete Marketing Campaign

Suppose we are an insurance company that wants to launch a marketing campaign to generate new leads. The company launches a campaign on its website and proposes potential customers to get a free offer for their car insurance.

Each time a customer registers himself through the contact form, a lead is created in OpenERP. For further information about web contact forms, please refer to the chapter *Automating your Lead Acquisition* (page 89).

The salesperson responsible for Car Insurances triggers the marketing campaign by sending an introductory email of all the insurance services we offer and thanking for subscribing for the free Car Insurance Offer.

Based on the response, the insurance company plots whether the lead is interested in:

- Buying a Car Insurance,
- Information about other Insurance policies,
- Buying the book about Keeping your Children Safe.

According to the replies we receive from the leads, we send an email catering their respective needs.

- If they respond back to such an email, the lead is converted into an opportunity. When the lead buys a car insurance, the lead becomes our partner and is created as a customer in OpenERP.
- If we do not receive an answer, they get a reminder regarding the offer a week later. If they still do not answer, our salesperson gives a voluntary call to ask about their needs.

See it as a flowchart allowing us to trigger a respective activity for every possible cue. The chances of leads going unattended become very low, and for every lead, we have a predefined method of handling it.

Moreover, we can measure the method according to our goals. Based on the goals we can evaluate the effectiveness of our campaign and analyze whether there is room for improvement.

**Campaign Example**

To a get an example of a complete campaign in OpenERP, you can install the `marketing_campaign_crm_demo` module.

## 9.2 Designing your Campaigns

Designing a marketing campaign is mostly a long term process and the success of any campaign depends on the research and the effectiveness in selecting your target audience for the campaign. There are certain questions that every marketeer always asks while designing a campaign.

- What would be our marketing campaign?
- Who would be the target audience?
- How would we measure the effectiveness of our campaign?

The OpenERP campaign is based on the principle of *lead automation*. A lead is created according to a specific response by a customer towards a stimulus. An example: filling the car insurance calculator on your website may create a lead in OpenERP.

The first step is to define the campaign, i.e. the sequence of steps to be performed. By defining the campaign, we trigger a set of activities in the **Marketing Campaign** application of OpenERP.

From the lead automation, we define the sequence of steps we ought to follow, the modes of creating and processing these activities and the cost involved in this campaign. After each activity and based on its respective stimuli, we can trigger the next event of the campaign concerned.

## 9.3 Segmenting your Campaigns

The two most important points for any successful campaign are the adoption of a concrete methodology of execution and choosing the right segment: a target loop of customers to whom our campaign would be directed (i.e. your target audience). Inappropriate focus on the wrong segment would result in the campaign being misfired and our efforts would reach deaf ears.

Through the *Segment* tab in the **Campaign** module, we can define our segment for each Campaign activity. Indeed, it is perfectly well possible that with every step downwards, the segment gets narrowed in terms of number. You can also synchronize the entire campaign steps according to the defined segments.

Our insurance company wants to attack the Spanish market, and will define a segment called Spanish Leads. Of course you would want your segment to be valid for leads coming from Spain only. To achieve this, go to the **Leads** list view. Filter all the leads for Spain (type *Spain* in the *Country* field), make sure to clear the salesteam, so that all leads coming from Spain will be selected. Then click *Save Filter* and call it for instance *Spanish Leads*. Now return to the **Campaigns** menu and open the *Segment*, then click the `Filter` field to select *Spanish Leads*. The segment will now only apply to Spanish leads.

As you can see, the **Marketing Campaign** module is closely synchronized with the **Customer Relationship Management** Business Application. Let us consider the segment we cater in the campaign as Leads in OpenERP. Goals are set for each campaign, which would be considered as a desired state. Once a lead meets our objective criteria of goals, we change the lead status by converting it into an **Opportunity**, meaning that we should give focused attention.

Once the lead satisfies our final objective, we would consider it as a partner/customer and close that lead.

## 9.4 Email Templates

OpenERP allows you to create your own email templates. You can use the Expression Builder to have the variables created for you. Suppose you would like to add the Contact Name in the email, but of course, this will be a different name for each email.

In the Expression Builder, in `Field`, select Contact Name. Automatically, the `Expression` will be filled. Copy the value from the expression and paste it in your email, e.g. Dear ${object.contact_name}. So your email will start with Dear followed by the name of the contact. This way you automatically create personalized emails.

For each email template, you can have OpenERP generate a Wizard Action / Button that will be related to the object. So if you choose to do marketing campaigns for leads, the action will be added to the right side panel of the **Lead** form.

**Configuring Marketing Campaigns**

Please notice that it requires some technical knowledge to configure Marketing Campaigns. To be able to see, create, edit campaign, users need to be in the *Marketing / User* group.

## 9.5 Setting up your Marketing Campaigns

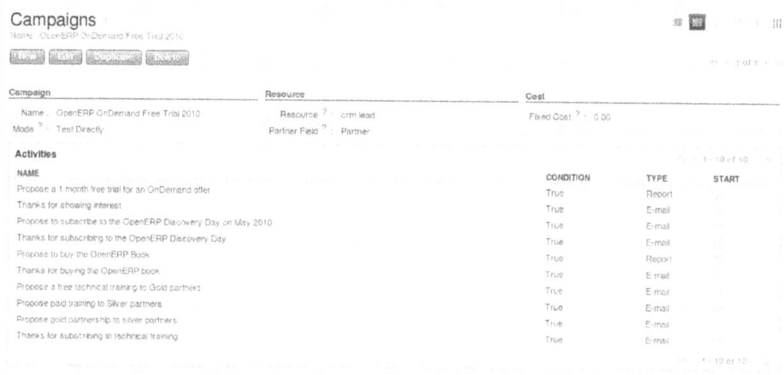


Figure 9.2: *Marketing Campaign*

0. Introduction

A campaign defines a workflow of activities that items/objects entering the campaign will go through. Items are selected by segments. Segments are automatically processed every few hours and inject new items into the campaign, according to a given set of criteria. It is possible to watch the campaign as it is running, by following the campaign "workitems". A workitem represents a given object/item passing through a given campaign activity. See it as a step that still can go either way. Workitems are left behind when the item proceeds to the next activities. This allows an easy analysis and reporting on the running campaign. Each activity may execute an action upon activation depending on a dynamic condition. When the condition is not met, the workitem is cancelled/deleted; if the condition is met, the action is executed, the workitem is marked as Done, and propagated to the next activities.

1. Campaigns (*Marketing → Campaigns → Campaigns*)

**Campaign** Each campaign is made of activities and transitions, and must be defined on any specific object the system knows about (e.g. Leads, Opportunities, Employees, Partners).

**Mode**

A campaign can be in one of 4 modes:

- *Test Directly*: processes the whole campaign in one go, ignoring any delay put on transitions, and does not actually execute the actions, so the result is simply the set of corresponding campaign workitems (see below). Any time a segment adds new items in the campaign they will be processed in the same manner.
- *Test in Real time*: processes the campaign but does not actually execute the actions, so the result is simply the set of corresponding campaign workitems. Any time a segment adds new items in the campaign they will be processed in the same manner.
- *Manual confirmation*: No action will be executed automatically, a human intervention is needed to let workitems proceed into the flow. It is like a step-by-step manual process using the Campaign Followup menu. You can ignore the time delays and force any step of the campaign, implementing the campaign at your pace i.e. (you have a test email and want to see if the steps and templates do exactly what you want them to do). You will see that the actions set are defined as To Do and Done and the page has to be refreshed to see the next activities defined by the campaign node: the campaign sends real messages to the actual targets, be warned.
- *Normal*: the campaign is processed normally, all actions are executed automatically at the scheduled date. Pay attention that in this status, the campaign sends real messages to the actual target audience.

Regardless of the current mode of the campaign, any workitem can be manually executed or cancelled at any time (even if it is scheduled in the future) through *Campaign Followup*.

**Resource** Specifies where the campaign will get the information from, i.e. the OpenERP object linked (e.g. Leads, Opportunities, Employees, Partners).

**Activities** Activities are steps in the campaign. Each activity is optionally linked to previous and next activities through transitions.

Each activity has:

- one optional condition that stops the campaign,
- one action to be executed when the activity is activated and the condition is True (could be a 'do nothing' action),

* one optional signal (ignore it),
* a start flag.

*Start Activity*

Activities that have the Start checkbox set, will receive a new workitem corresponding to each new resource/object entering the campaign. It is possible to have more than one Start Activity, but not less than one.

*Activity Conditions*

[a Boolean expression, made of clauses combined using boolean operators: AND, OR, NOT] Each condition is the criterion that decides whether the activity is going to be activated for a given workitem, or just cancelled. It is an arbitrary expression composed of simple tests on attributes of the object, possibly combined using *or*, *and* & *not* operators.

See section 6.1 for more information on Comparators.

The individual tests can use the "object" name to refer to the object/resource it originates from (e.g the lead), using a "dot notation" to refer to its attributes. Some examples on a CRM Lead resource:

* object.name == 'Insurance Offer Lead' would select only leads whose title is exactly "Insurance Offer Lead",
* object.state == 'pending' would select Pending leads only,
* object.country_id.code == 'be' would select leads whose country field is set to Belgium,
* object.country_id.name == 'Belgium' would select leads whose country field is set to Belgium.

Tests can also use a 'workitem' name to refer to the actual item denoting the position of the object in the campaign. This can be useful to access some specific attributes, such as the segment that selected this item. Some examples:

* workitem.segment_id.name == 'Insurance Offer EU Zone1 - Industry Consulting/Technology' would select leads that entered this campaign through the "Insurance Offer Lead EU Zone1 - Industry Consulting/Technology" segment,
* 'EU Zone1' in workitem.segment_id.name would select only leads that entered the campaign through a segment that has "EU Zone1" in its name.

**Help**

In the GTK client you can use "Help > Enable Debug mode tooltips" to see the attribute name of every field in a form. These are the same that you can use during import/export with CSV files.

You can also use the special formula re.search(PATTERN_TO_SEARCH, ATTRIBUTE_TO_SEARCH) where PATTERN_TO_SEARCH is a character string delimited with quotes, and ATTRIBUTE_TO_SEARCH uses the dot notation above to refer to a field of the object. An example for CRM leads:

- re.search('Plan to buy: True', object.description) would be true if the Notes on a Lead contain this text: "Plan to buy: True". Be careful that all spaces etc. do matter, so you may use the special pattern characters as detailed at the bottom to account for small variations,
- re.search('Plan to.*True', object.description) would be true if the Notes on a Lead contain this text: "Plan to" followed later on by "True".

You can combine individual tests using boolean operators and parentheses. Some examples on a CRM Lead resource:

- object.state != 'pending' and ( re.search('Plan to by:.*True',object.description) and not re.search('Plan to use:.*True',object.description) ) would be true if the lead is NOT in Pending state and it contains "Plan to buy", but not "Plan to use".

## 9.5.1 Guidelines for Creating a Campaign

- It is a good idea to have an initial activity that will change some fields on the objects entering the campaign to mark them as such, to avoid mixing them in other processes (e.g. set a specific state and Sales Team on a CRM lead being processed by a campaign). You can also define a time delay so that the campaign seems more human (note if the answer comes in a matter of seconds or minutes it is computer generated).
- Put a stop condition on each subsequent activity in the campaign to get items out of the campaign as soon as the goal is achieved (e.g. every activity has a partial condition on the state of the item, if CRM Leads stops being Pending, the campaign ends for that case).

2. Email Templates (*Marketing → Configuration → Email Template → Templates*)

Email templates are composed of the following information:

- The Email headers: to, from, cc, bcc, subject
- The raw HTML body, with the low-level markup and formatting
- The plaintext body

Headers and bodies can contain placeholders for dynamic contents that will be replaced in the final email with the actual content.

3. Campaign Segments

Segments are processed automatically according to a predefined schedule set in the menu *Administration → Configuration → Scheduled Actions*. It could be set to process every 4 hours or every minute for example. This is the only entry point in a campaign at the moment.

*Segment filters*

Segments select resources via filters, exactly the same kind of filter that can be used in advanced search views on any list in OpenERP. You can actually create them easily from any OpenERP screen allowing you to save filters. Save your advanced search criteria as a new filters and add them to the segment in the `Filter` field. Filters mainly consist in a domain expressing the criteria of selection on a model (the resource). See section 10.3 for more information on the syntax for these filters.

For Leads, the following filter would select draft Leads from any European country with "Plan for use: True" or "Plan for buy: False" specified in the body:

> **[ ('type','=','lead'),** ('state', '=', 'draft'), ('country_id.name', 'in', ['Belgium', 'Netherlands', 'Luxembourg', 'United Kingdom', 'France', 'Germany', 'Finland', 'Denmark', 'Norway', 'Austria', 'Switzerland', 'Italy', 'Spain', 'Portugal', 'Ireland', ]), '|', ('description', 'ilike', 'Plan for use: True'), ('description', 'ilike', 'Plan for buy: False') ]

6. Miscellaneous References, Examples

6.1 Reference of Comparison Operators:

- ==: Equal
- !=: Not Equal
- <: Bigger than
- >: Smaller Than
- <=: Bigger than or equal to
- >=: Smaller than or equal to
- in: to check that a given text is included somewhere in another text. e.g "a" in "dabc" is True

6.2 Reference of Pattern/Wildcard characters

- . (dot) represents any character (but just one)
- * means that the previous pattern can be repeated 0 or more times
- + means that the previous pattern can be repeated 1 or more times
- *?* means that the previous pattern is optional (0 or 1 times)
- .* would represent any character, repeated in 0 or more occurrences
- .+ would represent at least 1 character (but any)
- *5?* would represent an optional 5 character

6.3 Reference of filter domains

Generic format is: [ (criterion_1), (criterion_2) ] to filter for resources matching both criteria. It is possible to combine criteria differently with the following operators:

- '&' is the boolean AND operator and will make a new criterion by combining the next 2 criteria (always 2). This is also the implicit operator when no operator is specified.
  - for example: [ (criterion_1), '&', (criterion_2), (criterion_3) ] means criterion_1 AND (criterion_2 AND criterion_3)
- '|' is the boolean OR operator and will make a new criterion by combining the next 2 criteria (always 2)
  - for example: [ (criterion_1), '|', (criterion_2), (criterion_3) ] means criterion_1 AND (criterion_2 OR criterion_3)
- '!' is the boolean NOT operator and will make a new criterion by reversing the value of the next criterion (always only 1)
  - for example: [ (criterion_1), '!', (criterion_2), (criterion_3) ] means criterion_1 AND (NOT criterion_2) AND criterion_3

Criterion format is: ( 'field_path_operand', 'operator', value )

Where:

- field_path_operand specifies the name of an attribute or a path starting with an attribute to reach the value we want to compare
- operator is one of the possible operator:
  - '=' , '!=' : equal and different
  - '<', '>', '>=', '<=' : greater or lower than or equal
  - 'in', 'not in' : present or absent in a list of value. Values must be specified as [ value1, value2 ], e.g. [ 'Belgium', 'Croatia' ]
  - 'ilike' : search for string value in the operand
- value is the text or number or list value to compare with field_path_operand using comparator

## 9.6 Pushing your Campaign Results further

Of course, Marketing Campaigns can only be effective when you also do something with the results. OpenERP offers analysis features to help you better manage future campaigns based on the outcome of past campaigns. Learning from your results, that is.

The *Marketing → Reporting → Campaign Analysis* report allows you to analyse your campaigns in detail, both ongoing and completed campaigns.

Segments allow you to keep good track of the results of a marketing campaign. You can see from which segment you have most demands, for instance.

Thanks to good insights in the way your respondents answer to your campaign, you can continuously improve your marketing results!

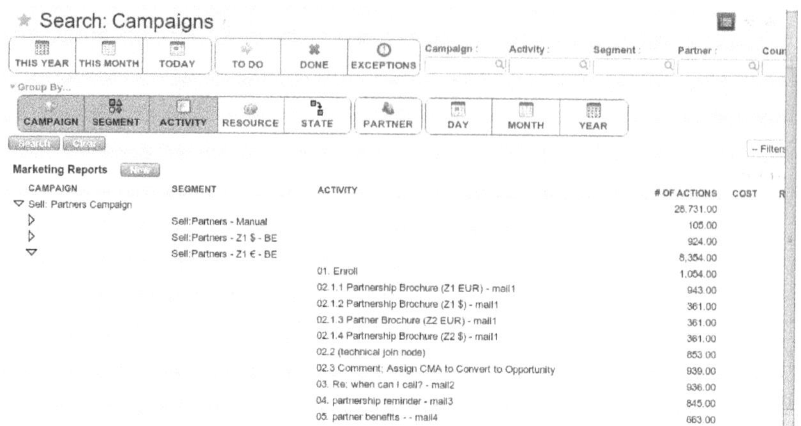


Figure 9.3: *Campaign Analysis*

# 10 Automating your Lead Acquisition

Through your website, your company wants to get as much information as possible about the people who visit the website. But how can you make sure that every person who wants to know more about your company is actually registered somewhere?

Well, you could use a Contact form for this. And precisely such a form allows you to register contacts automatically in OpenERP. By creating a link from your website's Contact form to OpenERP, your contact data will automatically be created in the CRM (or any other application of your choice, such as HR).

Let us show you an example of how this can be achieved. The figure below shows a Contact form on a website.

**Download eBook**

Buy the paper book on Amazon or fill this form to download the OpenERP ebook for free.

**About You**

| | | | | | |
|---|---|---|---|---|---|
| Firstname | | (*) | Lastname | | (*) |
| Company | | (*) | Jobtitle | | (*) |
| Email | | (*) | Phone | | (*) |
| City | | (*) | Zipcode | | (*) |
| State | | | Country | -- select an option -- | (*) |
| Industry expertise | -- select an option -- | (*) | No.of employees | -- select an option -- | (*) |

**Your primary interest with openerp**

› General interests about OpenERP

› Interest about implementing OpenERP within your company

› Interest about becoming a partner

→ Click here to leave us a comment...

Download OpenERP book

Figure 10.1: *Contact Form on your Website*

All data entered in this form are linked to the **Lead** form in the CRM. Each time someone enters this contact form, a new lead is automatically created in OpenERP.

Such a system is a very easy yet flexible way of keeping track of your leads and automatically launch your marketing campaigns.

## 10.1 How to Link a Web Contact Form to OpenERP?

OpenERP is accessible through XML-RPC interfaces, for which libraries exist in many languages.

*Python example*

import xmlrpclib # ... define HOST, PORT, DB, USER, PASS url = 'http://%s:%d/xmlrpc/common' % (HOST,PORT) sock = xmlrpclib.ServerProxy(url) uid = sock.login(DB,USER,PASS) print "Logged in as %s (uid:%d)" % (USER,uid) # Create a new lead url = 'http://%s:%d/xmlrpc/object' % (HOST,PORT) sock = xmlrpclib.ServerProxy(url) args = { 'name' : 'A New Lead', 'description' : 'This is a new lead from the web contact form', 'inventor_id': uid, } lead_id = sock.execute(DB,uid,PASS,'crm.lead','create',args)

*PHP Example*

<?php include("xmlrpc.inc"); // XMLRPC library file $xmlrpc_internalencoding = 'UTF-8';

$error="";

class Lead {

function createLead($usr, $pass, $database, $server, $data) { // Function for creating new lead in CRM

// Define variable which is used most frequently $user = $usr; $pass = $pass; $db = $database; $server_url = $server;

$client = new xmlrpc_client($server_url.'common'); // connect with server "common" services use for logging purpose

$msg = new xmlrpcmsg('login'); $msg->addParam(new xmlrpcval($db, "string")); $msg->addParam(new xmlrpcval($user, "string")); $msg->addParam(new xmlrpcval($pass, "string"));

$res = &$client->send($msg); // Send parse message to server and in response getting id

if(!$res->faultCode()){ // Check for error of response

$val = $res->value(); $id = $val->scalarval(); // Getting a value from response

**if (empty($id))**{ die("Connection error.");

} else {

$client2 = new xmlrpc_client($server_url.'object'); // Create second object for manipulation operation

// Make a structure of fields for sending data to server $val = array (

"name" => new xmlrpcval("".$data['company'],"string"), "email_from" => new xmlrpcval($data['email'], "string"), "phone" => new xmlrpcval($post['phone'], "string"), "partner_name" => new xmlrpcval("".$data['company'],"string"),

```
            "contact_name" => new xmlrpcval($data['firstname'].'
            '.$data['lastname'], "string"), "function" => new
            xmlrpcval($data["jobtitle"], "string"), "zip" => new
            xmlrpcval($data['zip'], "string"), "city" => new
            xmlrpcval($data['city'], "string")
        );
        // Prepare message for creating new lead on server $msg
        = new xmlrpcmsg('execute'); $msg->addParam(new
        xmlrpcval($db, "string")); $msg->addParam(new
        xmlrpcval($id, "int")); $msg->addParam(new
        xmlrpcval($pass, "string")); $msg->addParam(new
        xmlrpcval("crm.lead", "string")); $msg->addParam(new
        xmlrpcval("create", "string")); $msg->addParam(new
        xmlrpcval($val, "struct"));
        $res2 = &$client2->send($msg); // Send message using
        "object" services for new lead generation
        if(!$res2->faultCode()) { // Check for error of response
            $readVal = $res2->value()->scalarval(); // Getting a new lead id
            if (!empty($readVal)) {
                $caseid = array(new xmlrpcval($readVal, "int"));
                // Prepair a message for creating history $msg = new xmlrpcmsg('execute');
                $msg->addParam(new xmlrpcval($db, "string")); $msg->addParam(new xmlrpcval($id,
                "int")); $msg->addParam(new xmlrpcval($pass, "string")); $msg->addParam(new
                xmlrpcval("crm.lead", "string")); $msg->addParam(new xmlrpcval("history", "string"));
                $msg->addParam(new xmlrpcval($caseid, "array")); $msg->addParam(new xmlrpcval("",
                "string")); $msg->addParam(new xmlrpcval(true, "boolean")); $msg->addParam(new
                xmlrpcval("", "string")); $msg->addParam(new xmlrpcval("<From email id>", "string"));
                $msg->addParam(new xmlrpcval("< Description >", "string")); $msg->addParam(new
                xmlrpcval("<To email id >", "string")); $msg->addParam(new xmlrpcval("", "string"));
                $msg->addParam(new xmlrpcval("", "string")); $msg->addParam(new xmlrpcval("",
                "string")); $msg->addParam(new xmlrpcval("", "string")); $msg->addParam(new
                xmlrpcval("", "string")); $msg->addParam(new xmlrpcval("", "string"));
                $msg->addParam(new xmlrpcval("", "string"));
                $res2 = &$client2->send($msg); // Send message using "object" services for creating history
            } else {
                $error="Lead is not created";
            }
        } else { // If lead is not generated then return error message
            $error="system unavailable [" . $res2->faultString() . "]";
        }
    }
} else { // If connection is not made with server
    $error="system unavailable [" . $res2->faultString() . "]";
}
}
```

}

$arrData = array(); // Make an array(key, value) of post data foreach ($_POST as $var => $value) {

$arrData[$var]=is_string($value) ? trim(stripslashes($value)) : $value;

}

$cnt = new Lead (); // Create new object of lead class $cnt->createLead('<user>', '<pass>', '<database>', '<server>', $arrData); // Calling method of a class

?>

**How to Link a Web Contact Form to OpenERP?**

For more information, you can also refer to the Technical Memento that you can download from http://www.openerp.com/community, the chapter about WebServices – XML-RPC.

# 11 Profiling your Customers

The segmentation tools let you create partner groups (or categories) and act on each segment differently according to questionnaires. For example, you could create pricelists for each of the segments, or start phone marketing campaigns by segment. To allow you to work with segments in OpenERP, you should install the `crm_profiling` module, which can also be achieved from the Configuration Wizard (Marketing - Profiling).

Profiling can be used to qualify your customers according to a questionnaire you define. When you establish a good customer profile, this will surely help you to close your deals. Customer profiles might even help you beat your competitors!

## 11.1 Establishing the Profiles of Prospects

During presales activities it is useful to qualify your prospects quickly. You can ask a series of questions to find out what product / service to offer to the customer, or how quickly you should handle the request.

**Profiling**

This method of rapidly qualifying prospects is often used by companies who carry out presales by phone. A prospect list is imported into the OpenERP system as a set of partners and the operators then ask a series of questions to each prospect by phone.

Responses to these questions enable each prospect to be qualified automatically which leads to a specific service being offered based on their responses.

As an illustration, take the case of a software company which offers a service based on the OpenERP software. The company goes to several exhibitions and encounters dozens of prospects over a few days. It is important to handle each request quickly and efficiently.

The products offered at these exhibitions are:

- training on OpenERP – for independent people or small companies,
- partner contract – for IT companies that intend to offer an OpenERP service,
- OpenERP as SaaS – for small companies,
- a meeting in conjunction with a partner to provide a demonstration aimed at providing a software integration – for companies that are slightly larger.

The IT company has therefore put a decision tree in place based on the answers to several questions to prospects. These are given in the following figure *Example of Profiling Customer Prospects by the OpenERP Company* (page 94):

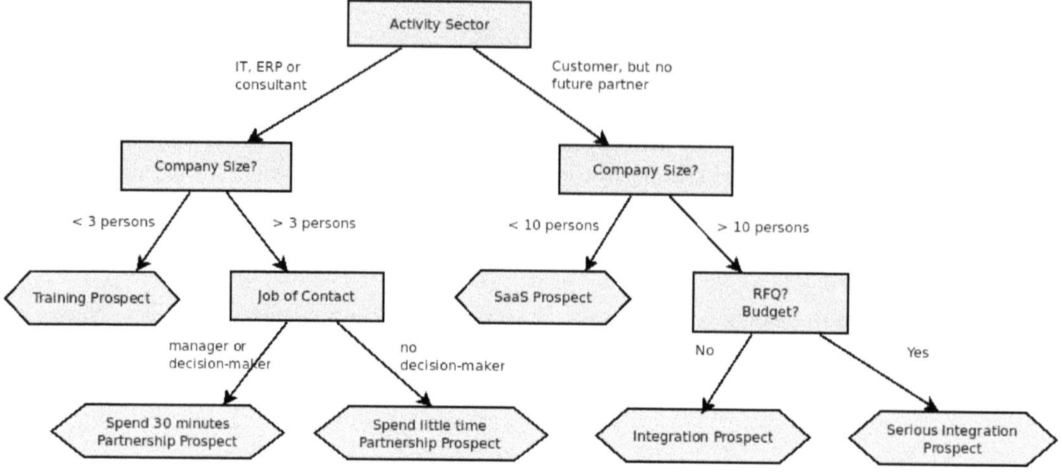


Figure 11.1: *Example of Profiling Customer Prospects by the OpenERP Company*

The sales person starts by asking the questions mentioned above and then after only a couple of minutes of work, he can decide what to propose to the prospective customer simply by analysing the prospect's answers.

At the end of the exhibition, prospects' details and their responses to the questionnaire are entered into OpenERP. The profiling system automatically classifies the prospects into appropriate partner categories.

This enables your sales people to efficiently follow up prospects and adapt their approach according to each prospect's profile. For example, they can send a letter based on a template developed for a specific partner category. They would use OpenERP's report editor and generator for their sales proposition, such as an invitation to a training session a week after the show.

## 11.2 Using Profiles effectively

To use the profiling system, you have to install OpenERP's `crm_profiling` module. You can also use the Reconfigure Wizard and add Marketing / Profiling.

Once the module is installed, you can create several questionnaires through the menu *Sales* → *Configuration* → *Leads & Opportunities* → *Questionnaires*. For each questionnaire, OpenERP allows you to create a list of questions and the possible responses through the menu *Sales* → *Configuration* → *Leads & Opportunities* → *Questions*.

To obtain the scheme presented earlier you can create the following questions and responses:

Table 11.1: Questionnaire for Defining Profiles

| Questions | Possible Responses |
|---|---|
| Journalist ? | Yes / No |
| Industry Sector ? | IT / ERP Consultant / Services / Industry / Others |
| Number of Staff ? | 1 / 2-20 / 21-50 / 51-100 / 101-500 / 500+ |
| Contact's job function ? | Decision-maker / Not decision-maker |
| Already created a specification for the work ? | Yes / Soon / No |
| Implementation budget ? | Unknown / <100k / 101-300k / >300k |

For instance, a sales person specializing in large accounts for the service sector could have a profile defined like this:

- Budget for integration: `Unknown` , `100k-300k` or `>300k` ,
- Already created a specification for the work? `Yes` , `No`
- Industry Sector? `Services` .

When entering the details of a specific prospect, the prospect's answers to various questions can be entered in the *Profiling* tab of the **Partner** form. All you have to do is click the *Use a Questionnaire* button on the *Profiling* tab of the **Partner** form.

OpenERP will automatically assign prospects to the appropriate partner category based on these answers.

Customers corresponding to a specific search profile can be treated as a priority. The sales person can access the profile of the large active accounts easily.

# Part IV

# Closing your Deals: from Quotation to Sales Order

# Creating your Products 12

The *Sales → Products* menu gives you access to the definition of products. In OpenERP, *product* is used to define a raw material, a stockable product, a consumable or a service.

**Consumables**

In OpenERP, a consumable is a physical product which is treated like a stockable product, with the exception that stock management is not taken into account by the system. You could buy it, deliver it or produce it, but OpenERP will always assume that there is enough of it in stock. Examples: nails, labels.

Open a product form to see its specific information.

Price lists (*Sales → Configuration → Pricelists*) determine the purchase and selling prices and adjustments derived from the use of different currencies. The *Default Purchase Pricelist* uses the product's *Cost Price* field for the Purchase price to be calculated. The *Public Pricelist* uses the product's *Sale Price* field to calculate the Sales price in quotations.

Price lists are extremely flexible and enable you to put a complete price management policy in place. They are composed of simple rules that enable you to build up a rule set for most complex situations: multiple discounts, selling prices based on purchase prices, price reductions, promotions on product ranges and so on.

To start, define the following product:

Table 12.1: Product Definition

| Field | Value |
|---|---|
| Name | Central Heating Type 1 |
| Reference | CCT1 |
| Product Type | Stockable Product |
| Supply Method | Buy |

From the menu *Sales → Product → Products*, click *New* to define a new product.

Three fields are important when you are configuring a new product:

- *Product Type*,
- *Procurement Method*,
- *Supply Method*.

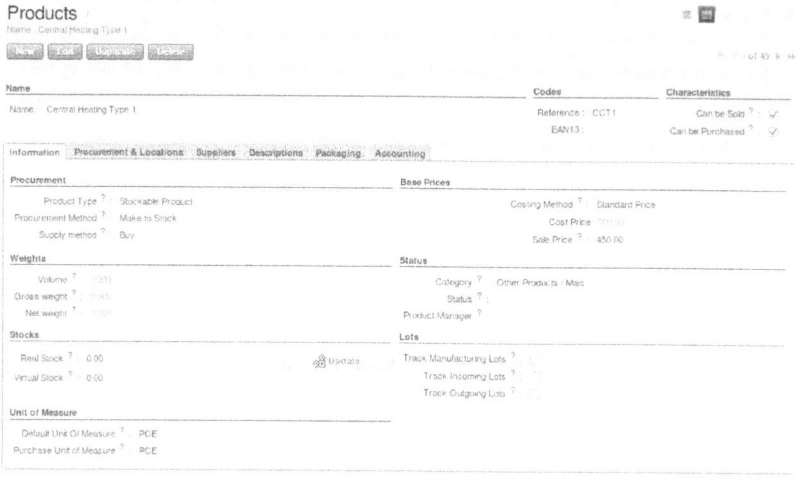

Figure 12.1: *Defining a New Product*

## 12.1 Using the Correct Product Types

The product type indicates whether the product is handled in stock management and if OpenERP manages its procurement. The three distinct product types are:

- *Stockable Product*: this product is used in stock management and its replenishment is more or less automated as defined by the rules established in the system. For these products, we have to know how many pieces we have in stock. Examples: a bicycle, a computer or a central heating system.
- *Consumable*: This product is handled in stock management, you can receive it, deliver it and produce it. However, its stock level is not managed by the system. OpenERP assumes that you have got sufficient levels in stock at all times, so it does not restock it automatically. Example: nails, labels.
- *Service*: It does not appear in the various stock operations. Example: a consulting service.

## 12.2 Procurement Methods – Make to Stock and Make to Order

The procurement method determines how the product will be replenished:

- *Make to Stock*: your customers are supplied from available stock. If the quantities in stock are too low to fulfil the order, a Purchase Order (according the minimum stock rules) will be generated in order to get the products required. Example: a classic distributor.
- *Make to Order*: when a customer order is confirmed, you procure or manufacture the products for this order. A customer order 'Make to Order' will not modify stock in the medium term because

you restock with the exact amount that was ordered. Example: computers from a large supplier assembled on demand.

You find a mix of these two modes used for the different final and intermediate products in most industries. The procurement method shown on the product form is a default value for the order, enabling the salesperson to choose the best mode for fulfilling a particular order by varying the sales order parameters as needed.

The figures *Change in Stock for a Make to Stock Product* (page 101) and *Change in Stock for a Make to Order Product* (page 101) show the change of stock levels for one product managed as *Make to Order* and another managed as *Make to Stock*. The two figures are taken from OpenERP's *Stock Level Forecast* report, available from the product form.

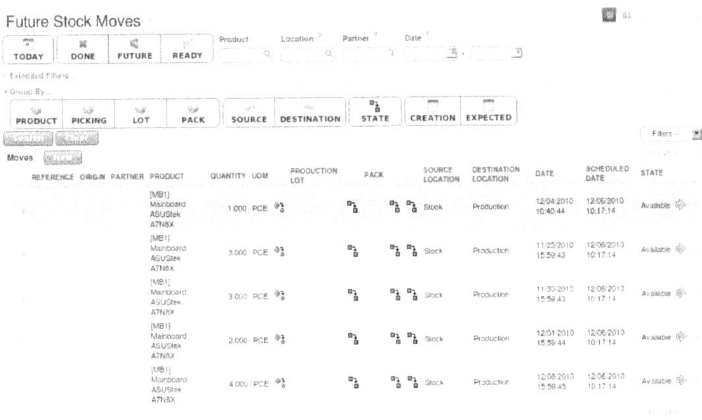


Figure 12.2: *Change in Stock for a Make to Stock Product*

Figure 12.3: *Change in Stock for a Make to Order Product*

**Logistical Methods**

The *Make to Stock* logistical approach is usually used for high volumes and when the demand is seasonal or otherwise easy to forecast. The *Make to Order* approach is used for products that are measured, or very expensive to stock or have a short restocking time.

## 12.3 Choosing Supply Methods

OpenERP supports two supply methods:

- Produce: when the product is manufactured or the service is supplied from internal resources.
- Buy: when the product is bought from a supplier.

These are just the default settings used by the system during automated replenishment. The same product can be either manufactured internally or bought from a supplier.

These three fields (*Supply Method*, *Procurement Method*, *Product Type*) determine the system's behaviour when a product is required. The system will generate different documents depending on the configuration of these three fields.

Figure *Workflow for Automatic Procurement, depending on the Product Configuration* (page 103) illustrates different cases for automatic procurement.

Figure 12.4: *Workflow for Automatic Procurement, depending on the Product Configuration*

## 12.4 Understanding Units of Measure

OpenERP supports several units of measure. Quantities of the same product can be expressed in several units of measure at once. For example, you can buy grain by the tonne and resell it by kg. You just have to make sure that all the units of measure used for a product are in the same units of measure category.

**Categories of Units of Measure**

All units of measure in the same category are convertible from one unit to another.

The table below shows some examples of units of measure and their category. The factor is used to convert from one unit of measure to another as long as they are in the same category.

Table 12.2: Example Units of Measure

| UoM | Category | Ratio | UoM Type |
|---|---|---|---|
| Kg | Weight | 1 | Reference |
| Gram | Weight | 1000 | Smaller |
| Tonne | Weight | 1000 | Bigger |
| Hour | Working time | 8 | Smaller |
| Day | Working time | 1 | Reference |
| Half-day | Working time | 4 | Smaller |
| Item | Unit | 1 | |
| 100 Items | Unit | 0.01 | |

Depending on the table above, you have 1Kg = 1000g = 0.001 Tonnes. A product in the `Weight` category could be expressed in Kg, Tonnes or Grammes. You cannot express it in hours or pieces, for example.

Use the menu *Sales → Configuration → Products → Units of Measure → Units of Measure* to define a new unit of measure.

In the definition of a Unit of Measure, you have a *Rounding precision* factor which shows how amounts are rounded after the conversion. A value of 1 gives rounding to the level of one unit. 0.01 gives rounding to one hundredth.

**Secondary Units**

OpenERP supports double units of measure. Notice however that the default unit of measure and the purchase unit of measure have to be in the same category. Only the sales unit of measure may be in a different category.

This is very useful in the agro-food industry, for example: you sell ham by the piece but invoice by the Kg. A weighing operation is needed before invoicing the customer.

To activate the management options for double units of measure, assign the group *Useability / Product UoS View* to your user.

In this case, the same product can be expressed in two units of measure belonging to different categories for sales and stock/purchase. You can then distinguish between the unit of stock management (the piece) and the unit of invoicing or sales (kg).

In the product form you can then set one unit of measure for sales and stock management, and one unit of measure for purchases.

For each operation on a product, you can use another unit of measure, as long as it can be found in the same category as the two units already defined. If you use another unit of measure, OpenERP automatically handles the conversion of prices and quantities.

So if you have 430 Kg of carrots at 5.30 EUR/Kg, OpenERP will automatically make the conversion if you want to sell in tonnes – 0.43 tonnes at 5300 EUR / tonne. If you had set a rounding factor of 0.1 for the *tonne* unit of measure, OpenERP will tell you that you have only 0.4 tonnes available.

The *Sales* → *Products* menu allows you to create new products and update existing products.

## 12.5 Categorizing your Products

Unlike partner categories (as explained in chapter *Categorizing your Partners* (page 28)) and their assigned partners, product categories do have an effect on the products assigned to them - and a product may only belong to one category. Product categories are linked to accounting and they determine the default income / expense account when invoicing. For a CRM point of view, categories will be very useful to group your sales information in a different way.

Suppose you would like to have product categories that correspond to your product lines (or your lines of business). With such a category tree structure, you can easily track your opportunities and forecast per product line. Go to the *Reporting* menu, and open the *Sales Analysis* screen to group your quotations and sales orders by category of products.

You can define new product categories from the *Sales* → *Sales* → *Configuration* → *Product* → *Products Categories*, and also directly from the *Product* form.

From the *Sales* → *Product* → *Products by Category* menu, you get an overview of all product categories according to their tree structure. To see the products linked to a particular category, simply unfold and/or click the product concerned. All products from that category will be displayed.

# Managing your Sales Quotations 13

In OpenERP, a quotation and an order are handled in the same form (a Sales Order), but in different states. You can consider an order to be a quotation that has evolved, because it has been confirmed by the customer. Or, conversely, that a quotation is an order that has not been validated or cancelled yet. Both your quotations and sales orders can be opened using the menu *Sales → Sales → Sales Orders*.

To enter details of a new quotation, you can use the menu *Sales → Sales → Sales Orders* and then select *New*. OpenERP opens a new window allowing you to enter data into a new blank quotation form. You can also create a quotation directly from an opportunity, as explained in a previous chapter.

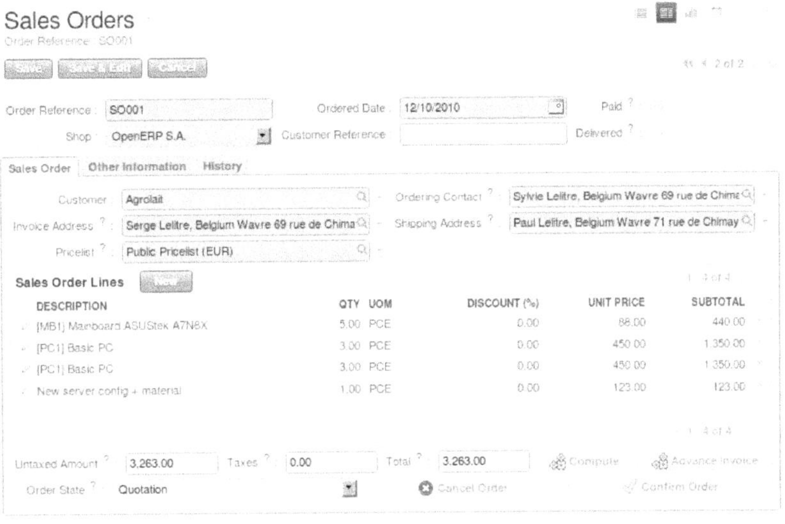


Figure 13.1: *New Quotation*

Some information is automatically specified by the system:

- an internal reference for the quotation or order,
- the sales point that the order will be delivered from,
- the order date,
- the pricelist for the current sales order.

You can modify any of that information before validating the quotation. The customer reference is shown in the header of the order. This optional field is for the customer's own reference – if the customer does not supply one, just leave it empty.

You then enter all the data about the order in the *Sales Order* tab. Start by entering the customer name, by selecting the correct customer from the list of customers in the system. From the quotation, you can create a new customer on the fly if necessary – press `<F1>` in the empty *Customer* field to do that, or type the name, press the *Tab* key and then click *Create*. Indeed, when you type a name or part of a name in the `Customer` field, and OpenERP does not find a corresponding customer, you will see the *Create* button appear to allow you to directly create the customer with the name you entered.

Once the customer name has been selected, different fields of the order are completed automatically, based on the configuration of the partner form for that customer:

- *Ordering Contact* : person handling the order at the customer end. By default, OpenERP proposes the Ordering Contact at the selected partner.
- *Delivery Address* : address used on the delivery order. By default, OpenERP proposes the delivery address from the partner form. If no specific delivery address is defined, the default address will be used instead.
- *Invoice Address* : address used to send the invoice to the customer. By default, OpenERP proposes the address labelled *Invoice* from the partner form. If no specific invoice address is defined, the default address will be used instead.
- *Pricelist* : will determine both the currency of the quotation and the price that will be used for each product.
- *Payment Term* : available in the *Other Information* tab, it shows the payment method that the customer will follow, for example `30 Days End of Month`.

You can modify any of these fields on the order as you go.

You can also set an analytic account for your order. This account will be used during invoicing to generate accounting entries corresponding to the invoice automatically. This is extremely useful for assigning revenues to the project or case specified by this order.

Once the information has been entered, you can enter data for the order lines. To do that, create a new order line as shown in the figure *Entering a New Sales Order Line* (page 109).

First of all, select the product that is to be sold to the customer. OpenERP shows some useful information in the list of products to help you making a sales quotation:

- *Real Stock* : physically present in your warehouses. This value depends on the Shop (sales point) selected in the order header. Different shops can be linked to different warehouses, giving different stock levels, or can use the same warehouse.
- *Virtual Stock* : shows a salesperson the quantity that can be sold, taking into account both stock reserved for other orders and the number of products planned to arrive in the short term.
- *Public Price* : the basic sales price for the given product. It provides a basis for the salesperson to be able to judge whether to offer a discount to the customer, and how much the discount should be.
- *Pricelist* : (may not be shown, depending on the installed modules) depends on the pricing conditions attached to the customer, calculated on the list price. This is the price that is proposed by default in the customer quotation, unless it has been modified by the salesperson.
- *Cost Price* : shows the cost price of the product. If the salesperson sells at less than this amount, the company incurs a loss.

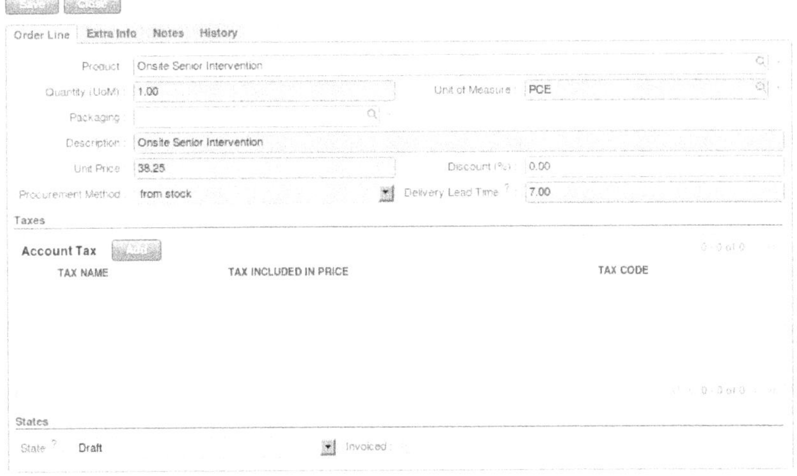


Figure 13.2: *Entering a New Sales Order Line*

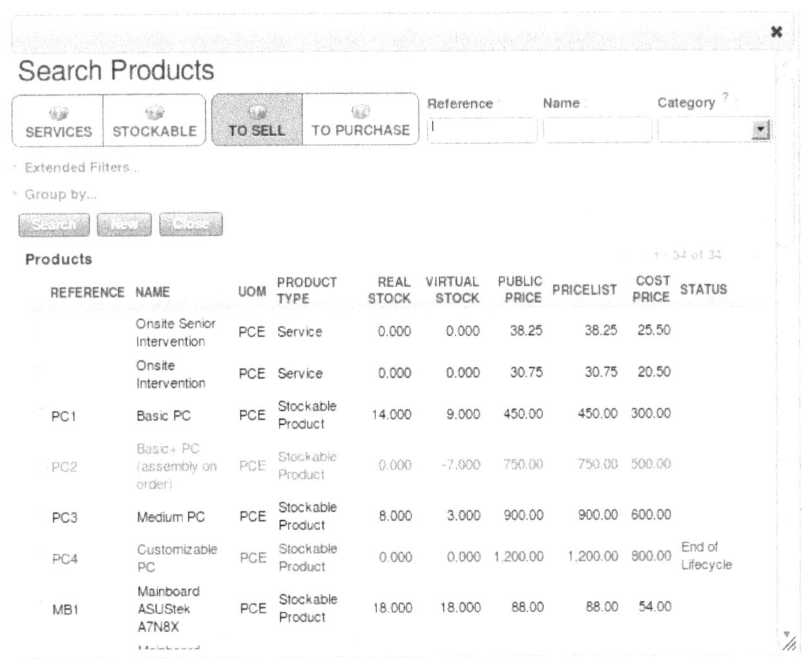


Figure 13.3: *Selecting a Product in a Sales Order Line*

Once the product to be sold to the customer has been selected, OpenERP automatically completes all the other required fields: quantity, unit of measure, description, unit price, discount, procurement method, lead times and applicable taxes. All of this information comes from the product form.

**Visible Discount**

If a discounted price is taken from a price list, by default that figure is shown as the sales price to the customer. He will see a discount of 0% along with the unit price that is different from the list price. If you install the module `product_visible_discount` from `extra-addons`, you can configure whether you want to make the discount explicitly visible in an order form as a percentage difference from the list price, or just show a reduced unit price as in the default configuration.

When you enter a quotation, the selected product is presented in the language of the user so that he can see what he is selling. The description of the product sold can also be expressed in the customer's language. The translation to the customer's language is used on the quotation or order when it is printed.

Figure 13.4: *Selling a Product in a Partner Language that differs from the User Language*

**One-off Sales**

If a product is sold to a customer only once, you do not have to create a completely new product form just for that sale. You can manually complete all the information in the order without actually creating a product: description, price, quantity, lead time, taxes. In this case, OpenERP will not generate a delivery note because the a pure description is not a product, and so it is not in stock.

When all of the products are entered, you can print the quotation and send it to the customer. To do this, click the *Quotation / Order* link in the *Reports* section to the right. OpenERP opens the quotation in PDF to enable to you to check it before printing.

When the order is confirmed by the customer, you can confirm the quotation to turn in into a sales order. You can also just cancel the window without confirming the order to leave it in quotation state. To see all the current quotations, you can use the menu *Sales* → *Sales* → *Sales Orders* and click the *Quotations* filter button.

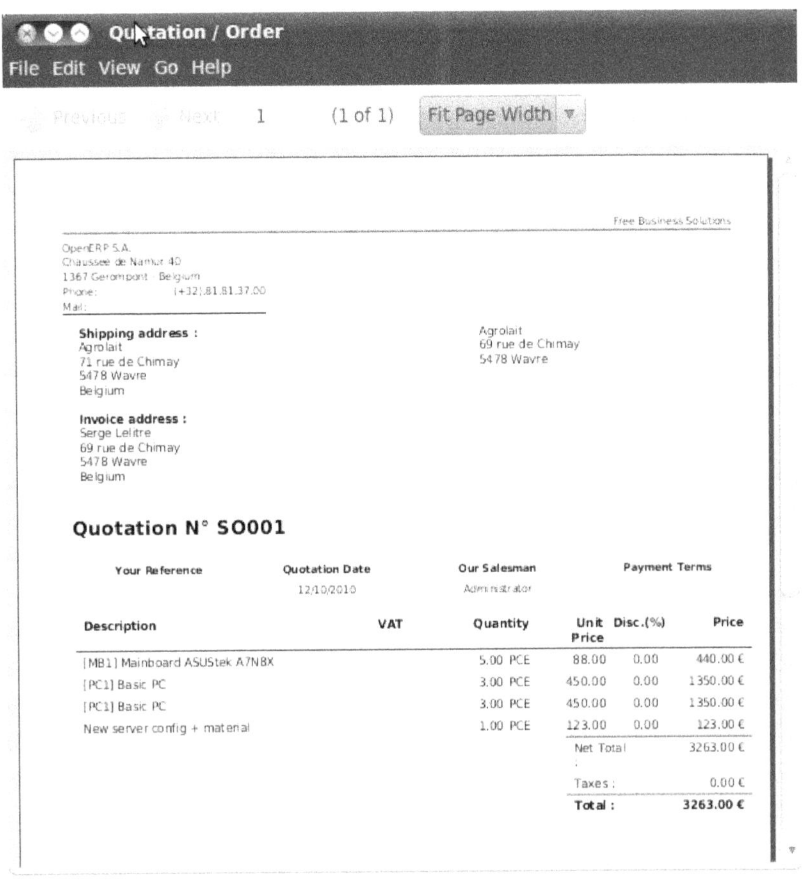

Quotation / Order

File Edit View Go Help

1 (1 of 1) Fit Page Width

Free Business Solutions

OpenERP S.A.
Chaussee de Namur 40
1367 Gerompont - Belgium
Phone: (+32).81.81.37.00
Mail:

**Shipping address :**
Agrolait
71 rue de Chimay
5478 Wavre
Belgium

Agrolait
69 rue de Chimay
5478 Wavre

**Invoice address :**
Serge Lelitre
69 rue de Chimay
5478 Wavre
Belgium

**Quotation N° SO001**

| Your Reference | Quotation Date | Our Salesman | Payment Terms |
|---|---|---|---|
| | 12/10/2010 | Administrator | |

| Description | VAT | Quantity | Unit Price | Disc.(%) | Price |
|---|---|---|---|---|---|
| [MB1] Mainboard ASUStek A7N8X | | 5.00 PCE | 88.00 | 0.00 | 440.00 € |
| [PC1] Basic PC | | 3.00 PCE | 450.00 | 0.00 | 1350.00 € |
| [PC1] Basic PC | | 3.00 PCE | 450.00 | 0.00 | 1350.00 € |
| New server config + material | | 1.00 PCE | 123.00 | 0.00 | 123.00 € |
| | | | Net Total : | | 3263.00 € |
| | | | Taxes : | | 0.00 € |
| | | | **Total :** | | **3263.00 €** |

Figure 13.5: *Printing a Sales Quotation*

To follow the process for your order, you can click on the process view (indicated by a question mark) from the order form. OpenERP shows you an interactive process view of that order. For more information about its use, look at the online documentation.

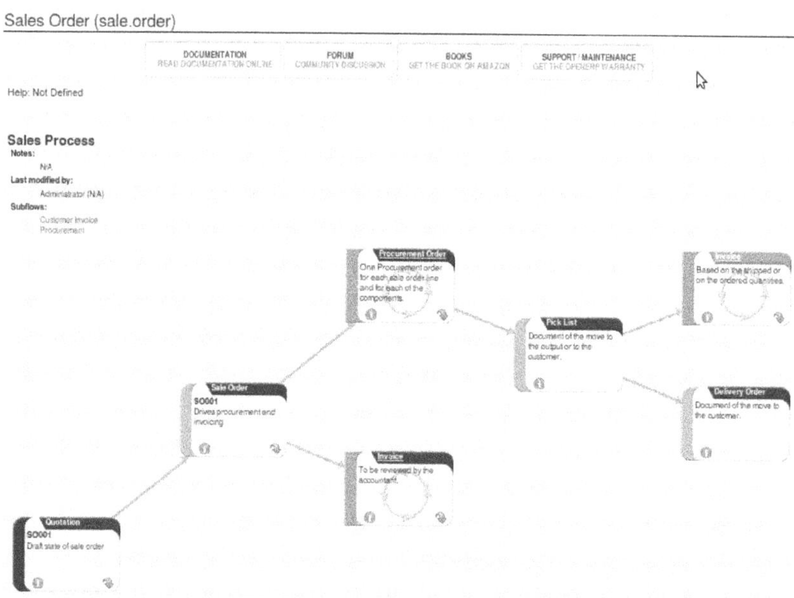


Figure 13.6: *Process View for a Sales order*

# Advanced Features 14

## 14.1 Defining Packaging

Products can be managed in several packaged forms. For example, if you sell batteries you can define the following packages for a given battery product:

- Piece: a battery,
- Blister Pack: a pack of 4 batteries,
- Pack of 100 blisters: 400 batteries,
- Palette: 40 packs for a total of 16,000 batteries.

OpenERP's package management enables you to sell the same product in several different forms. The salesperson could sell separately one battery or a palette of batteries. In the order, you can select the default packaging type as a function of the quantities ordered.

For example, if the customer wants to buy 30,000 batteries, the salesperson can select the `palette` package. OpenERP will then propose to sell 32,000 batteries, which corresponds to two palettes. Or the salesperson can select 75 packs.

The available packages are defined in the product form, in the *Packaging* tab. The first item on the list is the one that will be used by default.

Once a package has been defined on the order, OpenERP will throw up an alert if the ordered quantities do not correspond to the proposed packages. The quantity must be a multiple of the field *Quantity by Package* defined on the packaging form.

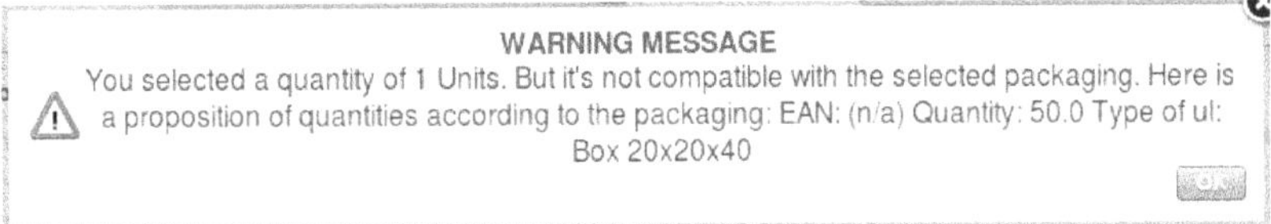


Figure 14.1: *Alert on the Quantities sold compared to the Packaging*

Do not confuse the management of packaging with the management of multiple units of measure. The Unit of Measure is used to manage the stock differently according to the various units. With packages, the stock is always managed by individual items, but information about the package to use is supplied to the storesperson along with that item.

Even if the effects are the same, the printed documents will be different. The two following operations have the same effect on stock movement levels, but will be printed differently on the sales order and the packing order as where quantities are concerned:

- 32,000 batteries, delivered on two palettes,

- 2 palettes of batteries, with no information about packaging.

If the customer wants to order a palette and 10 packs, the salesperson can put two order lines on the sales order using the same product with different units of measure.

It is sometimes more useful to define different products than to define several packages for the same product. A case of beer in a supermarket is a good example. A case holds 24 bottles, plus the empty case itself. The customer can buy bottles by the piece or a case of 24 bottles at one go.

You could define two packages for the `Bottle of beer`: `PCE` and `case` . But this representation does not let you manage the stock and price of empty cases. So you might instead prefer a Bill of Materials, defining and using three different products:

- the empty case for the beer,
- the bottle of beer,
- the case of 24 bottles of beer.

You also define the bill of materials below which determines the make-up of the case of 24 beers:

- Case of 24 bottles of beer: 1 unit,
- Bottle of beer: 24 units,
- Empty case of beer: 1 unit.

Each of these three products has a different price. The products `Bottle of beer` and `Empty case of beer` have a stock level that needs to be managed. The `Case of 24 bottles of beer` has no stock because, if you sell the product, OpenERP automatically moves the stock in two lines, one for the empty case and the other for the 24 individual bottles of beer.

## 14.2 Managing Alerts

To manage alerts on products or partners, you can install the `warning` module. Once that is installed, you will be able to configure a series of alerts on the partners or products by setting parameters in the new *Warnings* tab on each of the forms.

You can select any of the following types of warnings and create different warnings for purchases and for sales:

- *No Message*: This option will not display a message.
- *Warning*: This option will show the user the message entered.
- *Blocking Message*: The message displayed will cause an exception and block the workflow.

You can activate alerts for a series of events. For each alert, you should enter a message that will be displayed when the event concerned is started.

The available warnings in the partner form are:

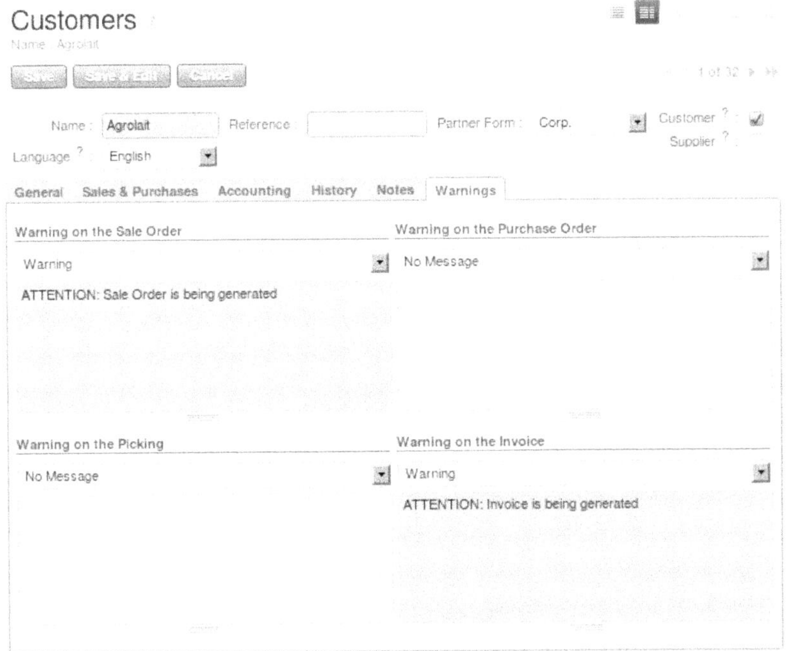


Figure 14.2: *Management of alerts on partners*

- Create a warning for a sales order,
- Create a warning for a purchase order,
- Create a warning for a delivery to a partner (or receiving an item),
- Create a warning when invoicing a partner.

For example, if you enter an alert for the invoicing of a customer, for an accountant entering an invoice for that customer, the alert message will be attached as shown in the figure *Alert from Invoicing a Customer* (page 116).

The alerts that can be configured on a product form are related to:

- The sales of that product,
- The purchase of that product.

A practical example:

Now when could you use such an alert? Suppose that your customer asks you to never make any deliveries on Tuesday morning, because the street is blocked due to a weekly market. You surely would like your transporter to be aware of this, so it could be useful to have a kind of message printed by default on each delivery order for this customer. To do this, you could create a Warning on the Picking in the **Customer** form of the partner concerned, saying that no deliveries are allowed on Tuesday morning.

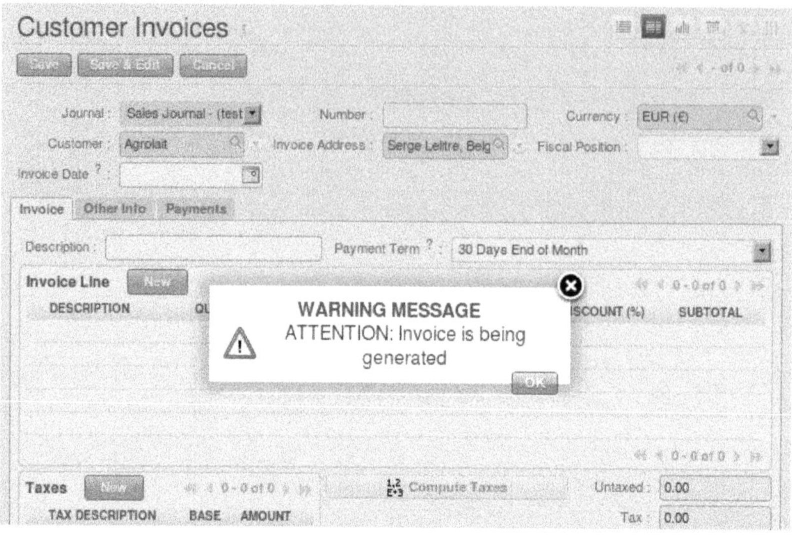


Figure 14.3: *Alert from Invoicing a Customer*

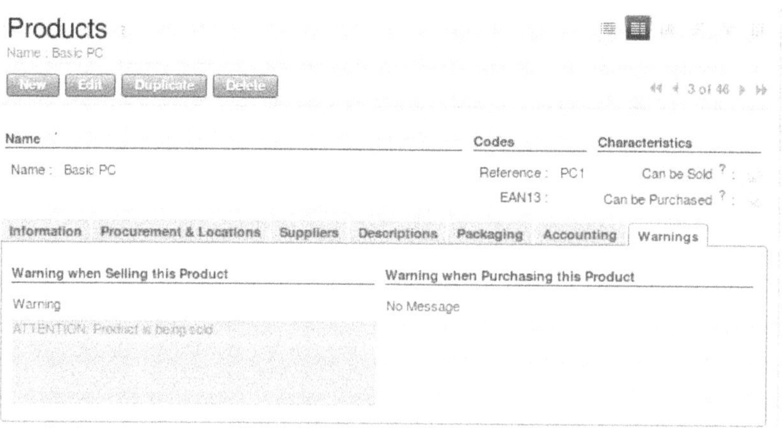


Figure 14.4: *Management of Alerts on Products*

## 14.3 Controlling Deliveries and Invoicing

### 14.3.1 Configuring Orders

The way the order is configured will determine its future behaviour:

- *Picking Policy* : `Partial Delivery` or `Complete Delivery`,
- *Shipping Policy* : `Shipping & Manual Invoice`, `Payment Before Delivery`, `Invoice on Order After Delivery`, and `Invoice from Delivery`,
- *Invoice on* : `Ordered Quantities` or `Shipped Quantities`.

**Configuring your Interface**

If you work in the `Simplified` view mode, only the *Shipping Policy* field is visible in the second order tab. To get to the `Extended` view mode, go to the *Edit Preferences* link and select the interface of your choice. You can also use the *Reconfigure* wizard and configure your interface as *Extended*, or assign the group *Usability – Extended View* to the current user.

The picking mode determines the way the storesperson will do the picking. If the order is put into *Partial Delivery* mode, the picking order will appear in the list of things for the storesperson to do as soon as any of the products on the order is available. To get the list of items to be done, you can use the menu *Warehouse → Outgoing Deliveries*. By default, the *Available* filter button is selected, so you immediately see the list of available pickings.

The storesperson will then be able to make a partial delivery of the quantities actually available and do a second picking operation later when the remaining products are available in stock.

If the picking mode is *Complete Delivery*, the picking order will not appear in the list of pickings to do until all of the products are available in stock. This way, there will only be a single delivery for any such order.

If the storesperson wants to do so, the delivery mode can be modified on each picking list even after the order has been confirmed.

In the case of invoicing from picking, the cost of delivering the products will be calculated according to multiple deliveries. This risks incurring a higher cost because of the separate deliveries. If invoicing is done from the order, the customer will only be invoiced once for the whole delivery, even if the delivery of several items has already been made.

## 14.4 Managing Carriers

To manage deliveries in OpenERP, you can install the `delivery` module. To do that, use the *Reconfigure* wizard and select *Delivery Costs* under the *Sales Application Configuration* section for installation.

This module enables you to manage:

- the different carriers with whom you work,
- the different transport methods,
- cost calculation and invoicing of each delivery,
- the transport methods and their tariffs.

Once the `delivery` module has been installed, the first thing to do is to configure the different modes of delivery accepted by your company. Go to the menu *Warehouse → Configuration → Delivery → Delivery Method* to create your company's delivery modes.

For each delivery mode, you should define the following elements:

- Name of the delivery mode,
- The partner associated with the transport (which can be your own company),
- The associated product.

Let's give you an example:

Table 14.1: Example Delivery Modes

| **Carrier** | **Carrier Partner** | **Delivery Product** |
|---|---|---|
| Express Track | Mail Office | Express Track Delivery |
| Priority Courier | Mail Office | Courier Express Delivery |
| EFG Standard | EFG Inc | Delivery EFG |
| EFG Express | EFG Inc | Delivery EFG Express |

Information about the invoicing of transport (such as accounts, applicable taxes) is entered in the product linked to the delivery mode. Ideally the product should be configured with *Product Type* `Service` and *Procurement Method* `Make to Stock`.

You can use the same product for several delivery modes. This simplifies the configuration, but it has the disadvantage that you will not be able to separate your sales figures by delivery mode.

### 14.4.1 Tariff Grids

Unlike ordinary products, delivery prices are not proposed through pricelists but through delivery grids, designed specifically for this purpose. For each delivery mode, you enter one or several tariff grids. Each grid is used for a given region/destination.

For example, for the postal tariffs for Priority Courier, you generally define the three tariff grids for Mail Office:

- National Courier,

* Courier in Europe,
* Courier Outside Europe.

To define a new delivery grid, use the menu *Warehouse → Configuration → Delivery → Delivery Pricelist*. Give a name to your delivery grid and define the region for which the tariffs in the grid will apply in the second tab *Destination*. There you can set:

* A list of countries (for UK or Europe, for example),
* A list of states,
* A range of postal codes (for Paris you might have 75000 – 75900).

Then you have to set the rules for calculating the transport price in the first tab *Grid definition*. First of all, give the rule a name. Then set the condition for which this rule is applicable, for example `Weight < 0.5kg`.

**Weights**

Weights are always expressed in kilograms. You can define a number with a decimal point or comma, so to set 500g you would put 0.5 in the weight rule.

Next you can set the sales price and the cost price. Prices can be expressed in various ways:

* a fixed price,
* a variable price, as a function of weight, volume, weight x volume or price.

For example, mailing within France using current tariffs would be defined as shown in the table below:

Table 14.2: Example Tariff Rules

| Name | Condition | Price | Price Type |
|---|---|---|---|
| S | Weight < 3 kg | 6.90 | Fixed |
| M | Weight < 5 kg | 7.82 | Fixed |
| L | Weight < 6 kg | 8.53 | Fixed |
| XL | Weight < 7 kg | 9.87 | Fixed |

You can also define rules that depend on the total amount on the order. For example to offer fixed price delivery if the total order amount is greater than 150 USD, add the following rule:

Table 14.3: Additional Tariff Rule

| Name | Condition | Price | Price Type |
|---|---|---|---|
| Franked > 150 USD | Price > 150 USD | 10 | Fixed |

## 14.4.2 Delivery Modes

Once the delivery modes and their corresponding tariffs have been defined, you can use them in a Sales Order. There are two methods for doing that in OpenERP.

- Delivery based on Ordered Quantities,
- Delivery based on Shipped Quantities.

*Delivery based on Ordered Quantities*

To add the delivery charges (or transport costs) to the quotation, use the button *Delivery Costs* available on the *Sales Order* tab of the form. A dialog box opens, asking you to select a delivery mode from the list available.

Figure 14.5: *Adding Transport Costs to an Order*

Once the delivery mode has been selected, OpenERP automatically adds a line to the quotation with the amount calculated by the delivery function.

If you want to calculate the exact delivery charges depending on the actual deliveries, you must use invoicing based on deliveries.

*Delivery based on Shipped Quantities*

To invoice the delivery according to the items shipped, you set the delivery mode in the *Delivery Method* field on the second tab of the order, *Other Information*, to *Invoice from Delivery*.

You can then confirm the order, and when the goods are available you can also validate the delivery order.

The transport costs will not be added to the sales order, but only to the invoice. When the manager has generated the invoices corresponding to the deliveries carried out, OpenERP automatically adds a line on each invoice corresponding to the delivery charge, calculated on the basis of the items actually sent.

# 14.5 Keeping Track of your Margins

For every company, keeping a clear sight on and a good control of margins is crucial. Even if you have a good sales level, it will not guarantee company profitability if margins are not high enough. OpenERP provides a number of methods allowing you to monitor your sales margins. The main ones are:

- Margins on a sales order,

- Margins by product,
- Margins by project (not explained in this book),
- Using pricelists.

### 14.5.1 Margins on Sales Orders

If you want to check your margins on sales orders, you can install the `sale_margin` module by selecting *Margins in Sales Orders* for installation in the *Reconfigure* wizard. This will add margins calculated on each order line and on the order total.

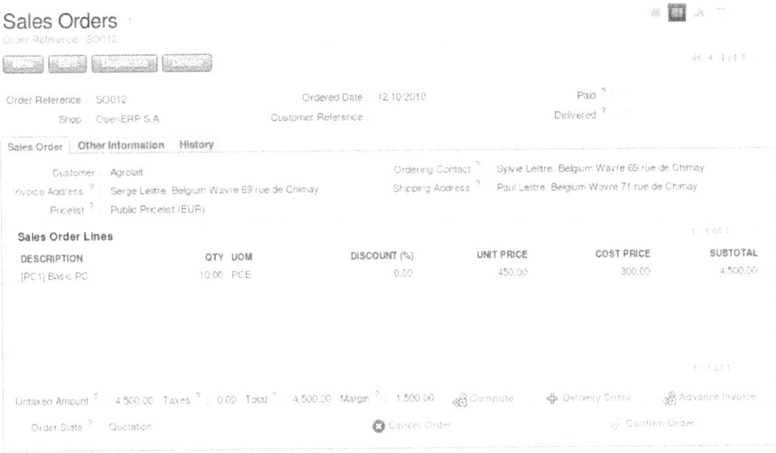


Figure 14.6: *An order with the module sale_margin*

The margin on each line is defined as the quantity sold multiplied by the sales price for the customer less the cost price of the products. By default, products are managed using standard price in OpenERP (cost price fixed manually and reviewed once per year). You can change that to `Average Price`, meaning that the product cost fluctuates with purchases from suppliers. After product receipt you can include fixed costs, such as delivery costs, in the cost of each product. OpenERP supports a third method of updating the cost price of products. This is through the button *Update* on the product form which lets you automatically recalculate the cost price for the selected product. The cost price is calculated from the raw materials and the operations carried out (if the products have been manufactured internally, so that you have set their costs).

### 14.5.2 Margins by Product

To track margins by product, install the module `product_margin`. Once the module is installed you can see the margins by product by using the menu *Sales → Products → Product Margins*.

When you have clicked the menu option concerned, OpenERP asks for an analysis period and the state of invoices (draft, open, paid). If no period is given, OpenERP will calculate margins on all of the operations without restriction. By default, however, OpenERP proposes a period of the last 12 months for analysis.

You can also filter the analysis on certain types of invoice:

- All invoices, including unvalidated draft invoices,
- All open and/or paid invoices,
- Paid invoices only.

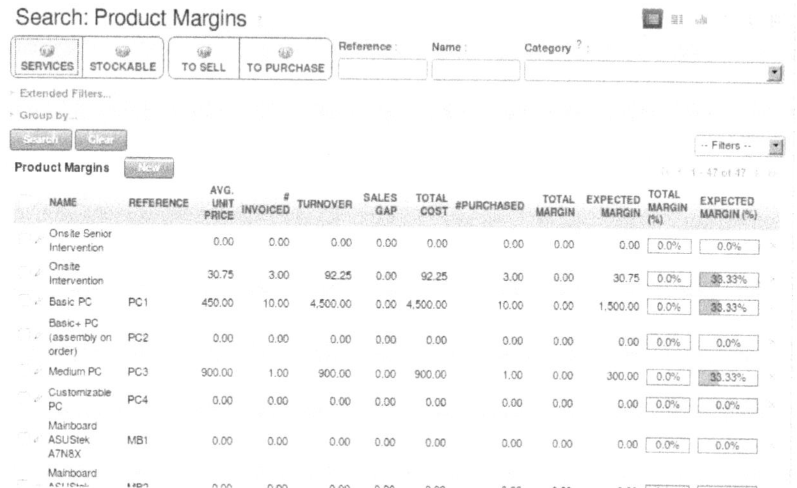


Figure 14.7: *Product Margins*

You then get a margin analysis table. The following fields are displayed for the sales of each product:

- *Avg. Unit Price*: the average unit sales price,
- *Catalog Price*: the list price based on this product,
- *# Invoiced*: the number of sold products that have been invoiced,
- *Sales Gap*: the difference between the revenue calculated from list price and volume, and the actual sales,
- *Turnover*: the actual sales revenue for the product selected,
- *Expected Sale*: the number of products sold multiplied by the list price.

The following fields are given by product for purchases:

- *Avg. Unit price*: the average unit purchase price,
- *Standard price*: the standard cost price of the product for the company,

Figure 14.8: *Margin Details for a Given Product*

- *# Invoiced*: the number of purchased products,
- *Purchase Gap*: the difference between the total actual cost and the standard cost multiplied by the number of units purchased,
- *Total Cost*: the total cost of purchases for the product under consideration,
- *Normal Cost*: the number of products sold multiplied by the standard cost price.

The following fields are given by product for margins:

- *Total Margin*,
- *Expected Margin*,
- *Total Margin in percent*,
- *Expected Margin in percent*.

## 14.6 Pricing Policies

Some companies are notorious for their complicated pricelists. Many forms of price variation are used, such as end-of-year refunds, discounts, change of terms and conditions with time, various prepayments, cascaded rebates, seasonal promotions, and progressive price reductions.

**Rebate, Refund, Reduction**

In some accounting jurisdictions you have to differentiate between the three following terms:

- Rebate: reimbursement to the client, usually at the end of the year, that depends on the quantity of goods purchased over a period.
- Refund: reduction on the order line or invoice line if a certain quantity of goods is purchased at one time or is sold in a framework of a promotional activity.
- Reduction: a one-off reduction resulting from a quality defect or a variation in a product's conformance to a specification.

Intelligent price management is difficult, because it requires you to integrate several conditions from clients and suppliers to create estimates quickly or to invoice automatically. But if you have an efficient price management mechanism you can often keep margins raised and respond quickly to changes in market conditions. A good price management system gives you scope for varying any and all of the relevant factors when you are negotiating a contract.

To help you work most effectively, OpenERP's pricelist principles are extremely powerful yet are based on simple and generic rules. You can develop both sales pricelists and purchase pricelists for products capable of accommodating conditions such as the date period, the quantity requested and the type of product.

**Do not confuse the Different Price Specifications**

Do not confuse the sales price with the basic price of the product. In OpenERP's basic configuration, the sales price is the list price specified in the product form, but a customer can have a different sales price depending on the conditions.

The same applies to the purchase price and standard cost. Purchase price is your suppliers' selling price, which changes in response to different criteria such as quantities, dates, and supplier. This is automatically set by the accounting system.

Each pricelist is calculated from defined policies, so you will have as many sales pricelists as active sales policies in the company. For example, a company that sells products through three sales channels could create the following price lists:

1. Main distribution:
   - pricelist for Walbury,
   - pricelist for TesMart,

2. Postal Sales.
3. Walk-in customers.

A single pricelist can exist in several versions, only one of which is permitted to be active at a given time. These versions let you set different prices at different points in time. So the pricelist for walk-in customers could have five different versions, for example: `Autumn`, `Summer`, `Summer Sales`, `Winter`, `Spring`. Direct customers will see prices that change with the seasons.

Each pricelist is expressed in a single currency. If your company sells products in several currencies, you will have to create as many pricelists as you have currencies.

The prices on a pricelist can depend on another list, which means that you do not have to repeat the definition of all conditions for each product. So a pricelist in USD can be based on a pricelist in EUR. If the currency conversion rates between EUR and USD change, or the EUR prices change, the USD rates can be **automatically** adjusted.

### 14.6.1 Creating Pricelists

You can define a pricelist from the menu *Sales → Configuration → Pricelists → Pricelists*.

For each list you should define:

- a *Name* for the list,
- a *Type* of list: `Sale` for customers or `Purchase` for suppliers,
- the *Currency* in which the prices are expressed.

#### PriceList Versions

Once the pricelist is defined you have to link at least one version. You can create a new version directly from the pricelist or from the *Sales → Configuration → Pricelists → Pricelist Versions* menu. The version contains all of the rules that enable you to calculate a price for a product and a given quantity.

Start by setting the *Name* of this associated version. If the list only has a single version, you can use the same name for the pricelist and the version. In the *Price List* field, select the pricelist you created (this is not necessary if you create the version directly from the pricelist).

Then set the *Start Date* and *End Date* of this version. The fields are both optional: if you do not set any dates the version will be permanently active. Only one version may be active at any one point, so bear this in mind when creating them. Use the *Active* field in the versions to activate or disable a pricelist version.

**Automatically Updating the Sales Pricelist**

Any sales pricelist can be set to depend on one of the other pricelists. So you could create your sales pricelist based on the supplier's purchase pricelist, to which you add a margin. The prices are automatically calculated as a function of the purchase price and need no further manual adjustment.

### Calculation Rules

A pricelist version is made up of a set of rules that apply to the basic product prices.

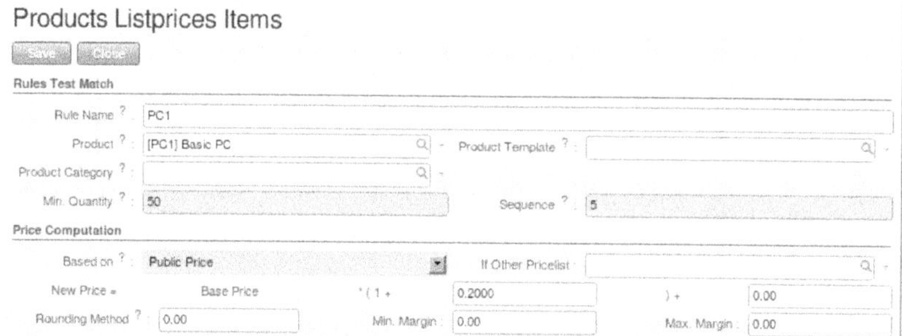


Figure 14.9: *Rule in a Pricelist Version*

You define the conditions for a rule in the first part of the screen labelled *Rules Test Match*. The rule applies to the *Product* or *Product Template* and/or the named *Product Category*. If a rule is applied to a category, then it is automatically applied to all of its subcategories too (using the tree structure for product categories).

If you set a minimum quantity in *Min. Quantity*, the rule will only apply to a quantity equal to or larger than the quantity set. This way, you can define reduced rates in steps according to the quantities ordered.

Several rules can be applied to an order. OpenERP evaluates these rules by sequence number, to determine which rule(s) to apply to the specified price calculation. If several rules are valid, only the first in sequence is used for the calculation. The *Sequence* field determines the order, starting with the lowest number and working up.

Once a rule has been selected, the system has to determine how to calculate the price from the rule. This operation is based on the criteria set out in the lower part of the form, labelled *Price Computation*.

The first field to complete is *Based on*. Set the way in which the partner price will be calculated, choosing between:

- the *Public Price* set in the product file,
- the *Cost Price* set in the product file,

- an *Other Pricelist* given in the field *If Other Pricelist*,
- the price that varies as a function of a supplier defined in the *Partner section of the product form*.

Next, various operations can be applied to the basic price to calculate the sales or purchase price for the partner, according to the specified quantities. To calculate it, you apply the formula shown on the form: `Price = Base Price x (1 + Field1) + Field2`.

The first field, *Field1*, defines a discount. Set it to 0.20 for a discount of 20% from the basic price. If your price is based on standard cost, you can set -0.15 to get a 15% price uplift compared to the standard costs.

*Field2* sets a fixed supplement to the price, expressed in the currency of the pricelist. This amount is just added (or subtracted, if negative) to the amount calculated with the *Field1* discount.

Then you can specify a rounding method. The rounding calculation is carried out to the nearest number. For example if you set 0.05 in this example, a price of 45.66 will be rounded to 45.65, and 14,567 rounded to 100 will give a price of 14,600.

The supplement from *Field2* is applied before the rounding calculation, which enables some interesting effects. For example, if you want all your prices to end in 9.99, set your rounding to 10 and your supplement to -0.01 in *Field2*.

Minimum and Maximum margins enable you to guarantee a given margin over the base price. A margin of 10 USD enables you to stop the discount from returning less than that margin. If you put 0 into this field, no effect is taken into account.

Once the pricelist is defined, you can assign it to a partner. Go to the Partner form and select its *Sales & Purchases* tab. You can then change the *Purchase Pricelist* and the *Sale Pricelist* that is loaded by default for the partner.

### Decimal Accuracy

There are several configuration settings related to the decimal accuracy of prices, or the number of decimal places to hold with each price field. To change the accuracy of a field, follow these steps:

1. Make sure you have the *Extended* user interface. The setting is in your user preferences.
2. Go to *Administration → Customization → Database Structure → Decimal Accuracy*. This list contains a number of predefined elements.
3. Open the entry you want to change. *Purchase Price* and *Sale Price* are the most common ones related to prices, but some fields are controlled by the *Account* entry.
4. Type a new value in the digits field, and save the entry. Do not change the description in the *Usage* field, or it will stop working.
5. Close the screen where you were editing prices and reopen it. The price field should now have the number of digits you asked for.

### 14.6.2 Example of a Pricelist

Take the case of an IT systems trading company, for which the following product categories have been configured:

All products

1. Accessories
   - Printers
   - Scanners
   - Keyboards and Mice
2. Computers
   - Portables
   - Large-screen portables
   - Computers
   - Office Computers
   - Professional Computers

In addition, the products presented in the table below are defined in the currency of the installed chart of accounts.

TABLE

Table 14.4: Examples of products with their different prices

| Product | Sale Price | Cost Price | Default supplier price |
|---|---|---|---|
| Acclo Portable | 1,200 | 887 | 893 |
| Toshibishi Portable | 1,340 | 920 | 920 |
| Berrel Keyboard | 100 | 50 | 50 |
| Office Computer | 1,400 | 1,000 | 1,000 |

#### Default Price Lists

When you install the software, two pricelists are created by default: one for sales and one for purchases. Each of them contains only one pricelist version and only one line in that version.

The price for sales defined in the Default Public Pricelist is set by default to the Public Price of the product, which is the Sales Price in the Product form.

The price for purchases defined in the Default Purchase Pricelist is set by default in the same way to the Cost Price of the product.

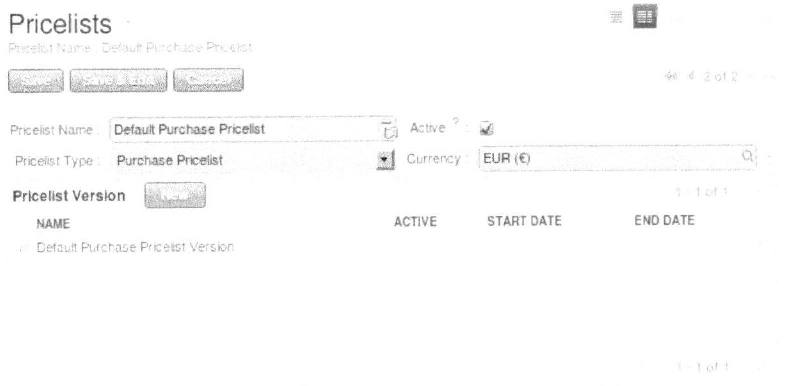


Figure 14.10: *Default pricelist after installing OpenERP*

### Trading Company

Take the case of a trading company, where the sales price for resellers can be defined like this:

- For portable computers, the sales price is calculated from the list price of the supplier Acclo, with a supplement of 23% on the cost of purchase.
- For all other products the sales price is given by the standard cost in the product file, to which 31% is added. The price should end in `.99`.
- The sales price of Berrel keyboards is fixed at 60 for a minimum quantity of 5 keyboards purchased. Otherwise it uses the rule above.
- Assume that the Acclo pricelist is defined in OpenERP. The pricelist for resellers and the pricelist version then contains three lines:

  1. `Acclo` line:
     - *Product Category* : `Portables`,
     - *Based on* : `Other pricelist`,
     - *Pricelist if other* : `Acclo pricelist`,
     - *Field1* : `-0.23`,
     - *Priority* : `1`.
  2. `Berrel Keyboard` line:
     - *Product Template* : `Berrel Keyboard`,
     - *Min. Quantity* : `5`,
     - *Field1* : `1.0`,
     - *Field2* : `60`,
     - *Priority* : `2`.
  3. `Other products` line:
     - *Based on:* `Standard Price`,

- *Field1* : `-0.31` ,
- *Field2* : `-0.01` ,
- *Rounding* : `1.0` .
- *Priority* : `3`.

It is important that the priority of the second rule is set below the priority of the third in this example. If it were the other way around, the third rule would always be applied, because a quantity of 5 is always greater than a quantity of 1 for all products.

Also note that to fix a price of 60 for the 5 Berrel Keyboards, the formula `Price = Base Price x (1 + 1.0) + 60` has been used.

### Establishing Customer Contract Conditions

The trading company can now set specific conditions to a customer, such as the company TinAtwo, who might have signed a valid contract with the following conditions:

- For Toshibishi portables, TinAtwo benefits from a discount of 5% of resale price.
- For all other products, the resale conditions are unchanged.

The sales price for TinAtwo, called `TinAtwo contract`, contains two rules:

1. `Toshibishi portable:`
   - *Product* : `Toshibishi Portable` ,
   - *Based on* : `Other pricelist` ,
   - *Pricelist if other* : `Reseller pricelist` ,
   - *Field1* : `0.05` ,
   - *Priority* : `1` .
2. `Other Products:`
   - *Product* :
   - *Based on* : `Other pricelist` ,
   - *Pricelist if other* : `Reseller pricelist` ,
   - *Priority* : `2` .

Once this list has been entered, you should look up the partner form of TinAtwo again. Click the *Sales & Purchases* tab to set the *Sale Pricelist* field to *TinAtwo Contract*. If the contract is only valid for one year, do not forget to set the *Start Date* and *End Date* fields in the *Pricelist Version*.

Then when salespeople prepare an estimate for TinAtwo, the prices proposed will automatically be calculated from the contract conditions.

### 14.6.3 Pricelists and Managing Currencies

If your trading company wants to start a product catalog in a new currency you can handle this several ways:

- Enter the prices in a new independent pricelist and maintain the lists in the two currencies separately,
- Create a field in the product form for this new currency and make the new pricelist depend on this field: prices are then maintained separately, but in the product file,
- Create a new pricelist for the second currency and make it depend on another pricelist or on the product price: the conversion between the currencies will then be done automatically at the prevailing currency conversion rate.

## 14.7 Rebates at the End of a Campaign

If you want to provide discounts on an order, you can use the pricelist system in OpenERP. But we would not be writing about end-of-campaign rebates if no other solution was available. You can also work with end-of-campaign rebates or year-end rebates. The customer pays a certain price during the whole of the campaign or the year, and he will receive a rebate at the end of the campaign according to the sales made throughout the year.

Take the case of contract negotiations with a wholesaler. To get the best selling price, the wholesaler will ask you for a good deal and will sign up to a certain volume of orders over the year.

You can then propose a price based on the volume that the wholesaler agrees to sell. But then you do not have any control over his orders. If at the end of the year the wholesaler has not taken the agreed volumes, you can do nothing. At most you can review his terms for the following year.

Rebates at the end of a campaign can help you avoid this sort of problem. You can propose a contract where the price depends on the usual wholesaler's terms. You can propose a rebate grid which will be assigned at the end of the year as a function of the actual sales made. Install the `discount_campaign` module (in `extra-addons` at the time of writing) to generate rebates at the end of the campaign. Once the modules have been installed, you can configure your campaign using the menu *Sales → Configuration → Sales → Discount Campaigns*.

**Year-end Rebate**

Most companies use the term *year-end rebate*, where rebates are applied at the end of the year. But of course you can also define rebates for a campaign that lasts less than or more than one year.

A campaign should have a name, a refund journal (to create the credit notes at the end of the campaign), a start date, and an end date. After entering this information, you should describe the lines of the campaign. Each line can be applied to a product or a category of products. Then set the quantity of products sold from which the discount is applied, and the amount of the rebate as a percentage of the actual sales volume.

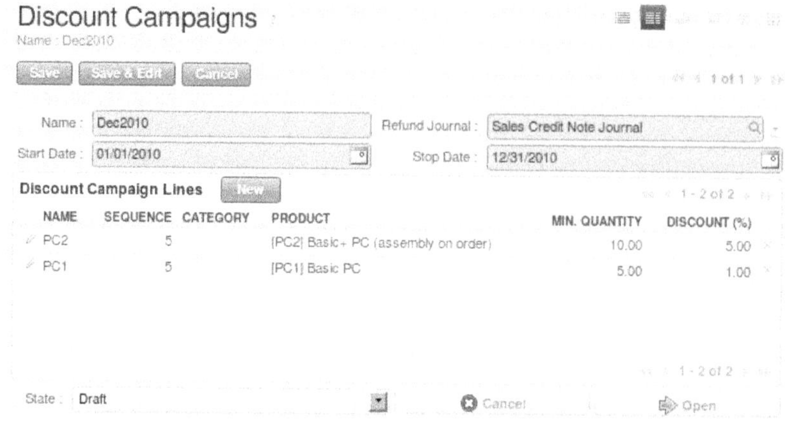


Figure 14.11: *Configuring a Campaign Rebate*

When you have defined the campaign, you can activate it by clicking the *Open* button. The figure *Configuring a Discount Campaign for Computers* (page 132) shows a campaign with a rebate on computers which is between 10% and 20% depending on the sales volume.

Figure 14.12: *Configuring a Discount Campaign for Computers*

Once the campaign has been defined and activated, you can assign it to various partners. To do that set a *Discount Campaign* in the second tab *Sales & Purchases* of the partner form.

Finally, at the end of the campaign, you should close it and OpenERP will automatically generate invoices or credit notes for your partner associated with this campaign. OpenERP opens credit notes in the `Draft` state so you can modify them before validation. To calculate the amount on the credit note, OpenERP uses all of the invoices sent out during the period of the campaign as a basis.

You can also get an overview of all draft credit notes using the menu *Accounting → Customers → Customer Refunds*.

## 14.8 Keeping track of Open Orders

In some industries, customers commonly place orders for a certain volume of products and ask for regular deliveries from an order up to the total amount on it. This principle, called open orders, is managed by the `sale_delivery` module in OpenERP.

OpenERP handles open orders easily. An open order is an order for a certain quantity of products but whose deliveries are planned for various dates over a period of time.

To do that, you should install the `sale_delivery` module (in `extra-addons` at the time of writing). A Sales Order is entered as a normal order, but you also set the total quantity that will be delivered on each order line.

Then you can use the new tab *Deliveries* on the order to plan the quantities sold and enter your delivery planning there.

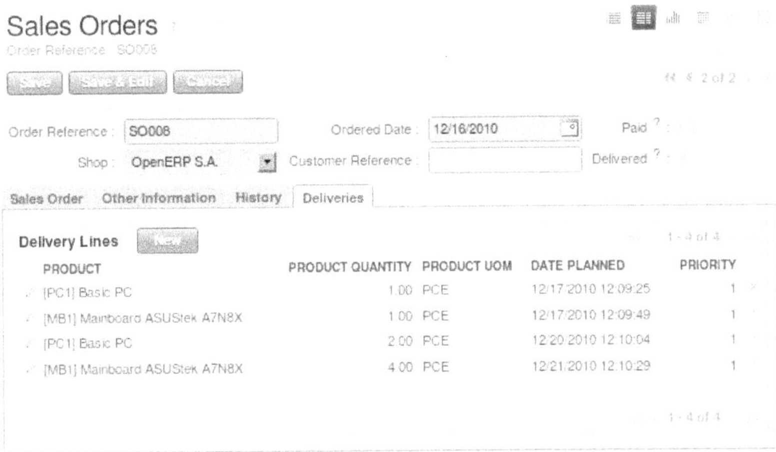


Figure 14.13: *Managing Open Orders, Planning Forecasts*

In the order lines, OpenERP shows you the quantity planned in addition to the quantity sold. This way, you can verify whether the quantities sold equal the quantities to be delivered. On confirmation of the sales order, OpenERP no longer generates a single delivery order, but plans scheduled dispatches.

**Invoicing Mode**

If you work with Open Orders, you should set *Invoice Control* to the mode `Shipped Quantities`. Then the storesperson will be able to re-plan and change the quantities of the forecast deliveries in the system.

## 14.9 Changing Order Layout

Install the `sale_layout` module by selecting *Sales Order Layout Improvement* and clicking *Configure* in the *Reconfigure* wizard. It enables you to have a more flexible template than the standard order forms.

For example, you could put the following in the order lines:

- a horizontal separator line,
- titles and subtitles,
- subtotals at the end of the section,
- comments,
- a page break.

This enables you to lay out a more elaborate, professional-looking quotation page. The module `account_invoice_layout` (installed automatically on installation of `sale_layout`), also gives you the same functionality for invoice templates.

The two figures *Invoice using Customizable Layout* (page 134) and *Printed Invoice* (page 135) show an invoice template in OpenERP and the resulting printed invoice.

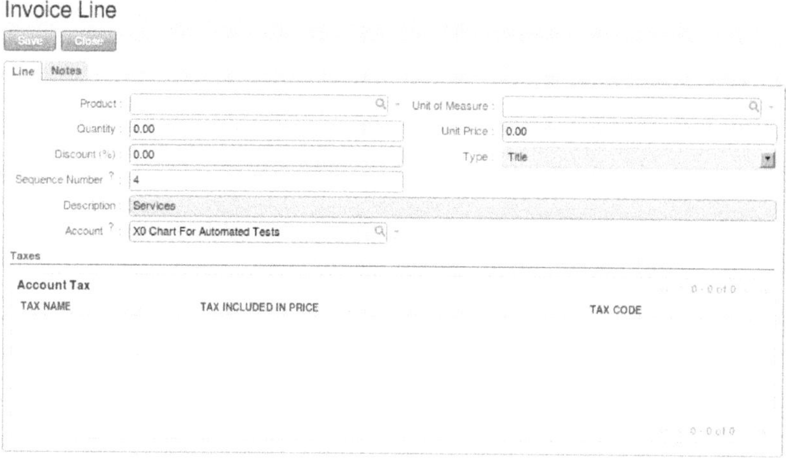


Figure 14.14: *Invoice using Customizable Layout*

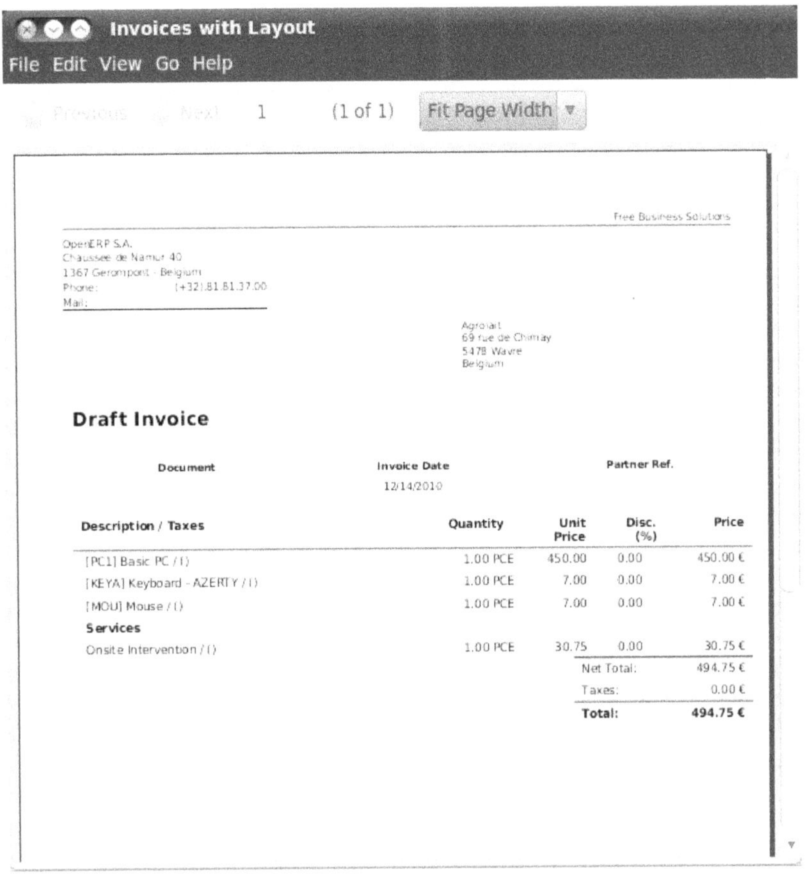

Free Business Solutions

OpenERP S.A.
Chaussée de Namur 40
1367 Gerompont - Belgium
Phone: (+32).81.81.37.00
Mail:

Agrolait
69 rue de Chimay
5478 Wavre
Belgium

**Draft Invoice**

| Document | Invoice Date | Partner Ref. |
|---|---|---|
| | 12/14/2010 | |

| Description / Taxes | Quantity | Unit Price | Disc. (%) | Price |
|---|---|---|---|---|
| [PC1] Basic PC / () | 1.00 PCE | 450.00 | 0.00 | 450.00 € |
| [KEYA] Keyboard - AZERTY / () | 1.00 PCE | 7.00 | 0.00 | 7.00 € |
| [MOU] Mouse / () | 1.00 PCE | 7.00 | 0.00 | 7.00 € |
| **Services** | | | | |
| Onsite Intervention / () | 1.00 PCE | 30.75 | 0.00 | 30.75 € |
| | | Net Total: | | 494.75 € |
| | | Taxes: | | 0.00 € |
| | | **Total:** | | **494.75 €** |

Figure 14.15: *Printed Invoice*

## 14.10 Invoice Analysis

Analyse your invoicing in OpenERP through the **Invoice Analysis** screen.

This report provides an overview of what has been invoiced to your customer as well as the average payment delays. You can easily group by partner, product category, ... or select only invoices that have not been confirmed yet.

This is an easy way to check your sales people's impact on turnover.

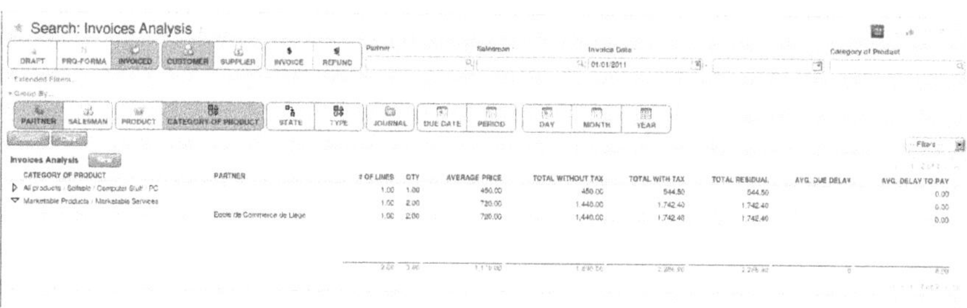

Figure 14.16: *Analyzing your Invoices*

# Part V

# Installing & Configuring your OpenERP

# OpenERP Installation on Linux 15

The installation procedure of OpenERP V6.0 is explained in this chapter. This procedure is well tested on Ubuntu version 10.04.

There are four main procedures that you have to follow in order to run OpenERP V6.0 smoothly:

- PostgreSQL Server Installation and Configuration
- OpenERP Server Installation
- OpenERP Client Installation
- OpenERP Web Installation

## 15.1 PostgreSQL Server Installation and Configuration

**Methods**

The PostgreSQL download page <http://www.postgresql.org/download/linux> lists the available installation methods. Choose the one that best suits your needs.

*Example on Ubuntu*

Use the following command on your system's command prompt to install the **postgresql** package:

```
sudo apt-get install postgresql
```

For example:

```
openerp@openerp-desktop:/$ sudo apt-get install postgresql
```

For a graphical user interface of **postgresql**, use the following command:

```
sudo apt-get install pgadmin3
```

For example:

```
openerp@openerp-desktop:/$ sudo apt-get install pgadmin3
```

You can find the new menu item **pgAdmin III** in your Ubuntu system menu from *Applications → Programming → pgAdmin III. Setup a PostgreSQL user for OpenERP*

When the installations of the required software are done, you have to create a PostgreSQL user. This user must be the same as your system user. OpenERP will use this user to connect to PostgreSQL.

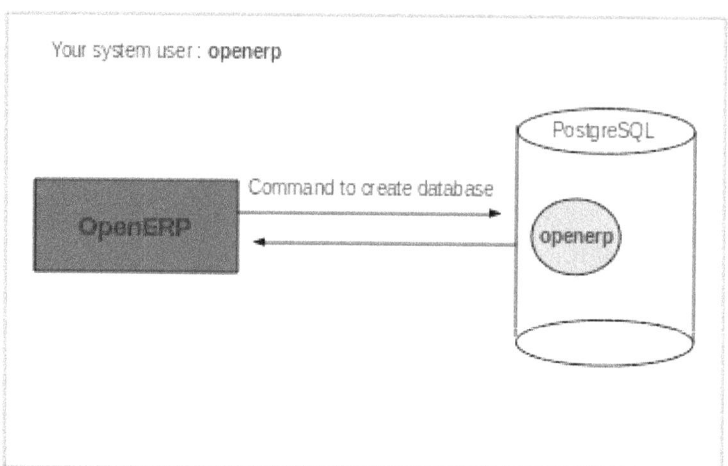


Figure 15.1: *Figure demonstrating how OpenERP uses the PostgreSQL user to interact with it*

**Database**

Without creating and configuring a PostgreSQL user for OpenERP as described below, you cannot create a database using OpenERP Client.

*First Method*

The default superuser for PostgreSQL is called **postgres**. You may need to login as this user first.

```
openerp@openerp-desktop:/$ sudo su postgres
password: XXXXXXXXXX
```

Now create PostgreSQL user **openerp** using the following command:

```
postgres@openerp-desktop:/$ createuser openerp
Shall the new role be a superuser? (y/n) y
```

Make this new user a superuser. Only then you can create a database using OpenERP Client. In short, **openerp** is the new user created in PostgreSQL for OpenERP. This user is the owner of all the tables created by OpenERP Client.

Now check the list of tables created in PostgreSQL using following command:

```
postgres@openerp-desktop:/$ psql -l
```

You can find the table **template1**, run the following command to use this table:

```
postgres@openerp-desktop:/$ psql template1
```

To apply access rights to the role **openerp** for the database which will be created from OpenERP Client, use the following command:

```
template1=# alter role openerp with password 'postgres';
ALTER ROLE
```

*Second Method*

Another option to create and configure a PostgreSQL user for OpenERP is shown below:

```
postgres@openerp-desktop:/$ createuser --createdb --username postgres --no-createrole
--pwprompt openerp
Enter password for new role: XXXXXXXXXX
Enter it again: XXXXXXXXXX
Shall the new role be a superuser? (y/n) y
CREATE ROLE
```

**Password**

Note that the password is *postgres*.

Option explanations:

- `--createdb` : the new user will be able to create new databases
- `--username postgres` : *createuser* will use the *postgres* user (superuser)
- `--no-createrole` : the new user will not be able to create new users
- `--pwprompt` : *createuser* will ask you the new user's password
- `openerp` : the new user's name

To access your database using **pgAdmin III**, you need to configure the database connection as shown in following figure:

You can now start OpenERP Server. You will probably need to modify the OpenERP configuration file according to your needs which is normally located in `~/.openerprc`.

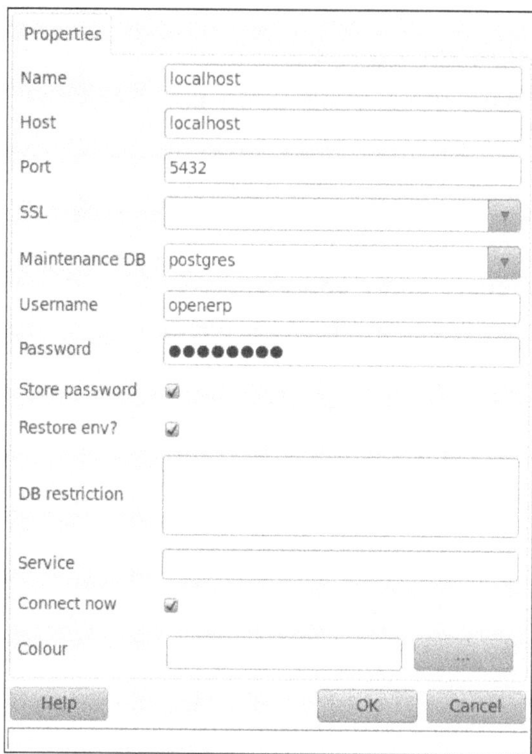

**Developer Book**

You can find information on configuration files in the Developer Book, section *Configuration*.

## 15.2 OpenERP Server Installation

*Installing the required packages*

You need to have Python (at least 2.5 for OpenERP v6.0) in your Ubuntu system, which is in-built in Ubuntu version 10.04 and above.

You also need to install the following Python libraries, because OpenERP Server uses these packages.

To install the required libraries on your Ubuntu system, you can do the following in your favourite shell:

- *lxml* : lxml is the most feature-rich and easy-to-use library for working with XML and HTML in the Python language.

```
sudo apt-get install python-lxml
```

- *mako* : Hyperfast and lightweight templating for the Python platform.

```
sudo apt-get install python-mako
```

- *mxdatetime* : Provides the most natural and robust way of dealing with date/time values in Python.

```
sudo apt-get install python-egenix-mxdatetime
```

- *python-dateutil* : The dateutil module provides powerful extensions to the standard datetime module, available in Python 2.3+.

```
sudo apt-get install python-dateutil
```

- *psycopg2* : Psycopg is the most popular PostgreSQL adapter for the Python programming language.

```
sudo apt-get install python-psycopg2
```

- *pychart* : PyChart is a Python library for creating high quality Encapsulated Postscript, PDF, PNG, or SVG charts.

```
sudo apt-get install python-pychart
```

- *pydot* : This module provides a full interface to create, handle, modify and process graphs in Graphviz's dot language.

```
sudo apt-get install python-pydot
```

- *pytz* : World Timezone Definitions for Python.

```
sudo apt-get install python-tz
```

- *reportlab* : The ReportLab Toolkit is the time-proven, ultra-robust, open-source engine for programmatically creating PDF documents and forms the foundation of RML. It also contains a library for creating platform-independent vector graphics. It is a fast, flexible, cross-platform solution written in Python.

```
sudo apt-get install python-reportlab
```

- *pyyaml* : PyYAML is a YAML parser and emitter for Python.

```
sudo apt-get install python-yaml
```

- *vobject* : VObject simplifies the process of parsing and creating iCalendar and vCard objects.

```
sudo apt-get install python-vobject
```

*Downloading the OpenERP Server*

The OpenERP server can be downloaded from the OpenERP website's download page <http://www.openerp.com/downloads>.

*Testing the OpenERP Server*

If you only want to test the server, you do not need to install it. Just unpack the archive and start the openerp-server executable:

```
tar -xzf openerp-server-6.0.0.tar.gz
cd openerp-server-6.0.0/bin
python openerp-server.py
```

The list of available command line parameters can be obtained with the `-h` command-line switch:

```
python openerp-server.py -h
```

*Installing the OpenERP Server*

The OpenERP Server can be installed very easily using the *setup.py* file:

```
tar -xzf openerp-server-6.0.0.tar.gz
cd openerp-server-6.0.0
sudo python setup.py install
```

If your PostgreSQL server is up and running, you can now run the server using the following command:

```
openerp-server
```

If you do not already have a PostgreSQL server up and running, you can read *PostgreSQL Server Installation and Configuration* (page 139).

You can find the OpenERP server configuration file at `~/openerp-server-6.0.0/doc/openerp-serve`

## 15.3 OpenERP Client Installation

*Installing the required packages*

You need to have Python (at least 2.5 for OpenERP v6.0) in your Ubuntu system, which is in-built in Ubuntu version 10.04 and above.

You also need to install the following Python libraries, because OpenERP Client uses these packages.

To install the required libraries on your Ubuntu system, you can do the following in your favourite shell:

* *gtk* : GTK+ is a highly usable, feature-rich toolkit for creating graphical user interfaces which boosts cross-platform compatibility and an easy-to-use API.

```
sudo apt-get install python-gtk2
```

* *glade* : Glade is a RAD tool to enable quick & easy development of user interfaces for the GTK+ toolkit and the GNOME desktop environment.

```
sudo apt-get install python-glade2
```

* *matplotlib* : matplotlib is a Python 2D plotting library which produces publication quality figures in a variety of hard-copy formats and interactive environments across platforms.

```
sudo apt-get install python-matplotlib
```

* *mxdatetime* : Provides the most natural and robust way of dealing with date/time values in Python.

```
sudo apt-get install python-egenix-mxdatetime
```

* *xml* : XML support for Python platform.

```
sudo apt-get install python-xml
```

* *tz* : World Timezone definitions for Python.

```
sudo apt-get install python-tz
```

* *hippocanvas* : The Hippo Canvas is a Cairo/GObject/GTK+ based canvas, written in C with support for flexible layout, CSS styling, and initial work on animations.

```
sudo apt-get install python-hippocanvas
```

* *pydot* : Python interface to Graphviz's Dot language.

```
sudo apt-get install python-pydot
```

**PDF Viewer**

You will also need a PDF viewer (e.g. xpdf, acroread, kpdf). See *Configuring a PDF Viewer* below.

*Downloading the OpenERP Client*

The OpenERP client can be downloaded from OpenERP website's download page <http://www.openerp.com/downloads>.

*Testing the OpenERP Client*

If you only want to test the client, you do not need to install it. Just unpack the archive and start the openerp-client executable:

```
tar -xzf openerp-client-6.0.0.tar.gz
cd openerp-client-6.0.0/bin
python openerp-client.py
```

The list of available command line parameters can be obtained with the `-h` command-line switch:

```
python openerp-client.py -h
```

*Installing the OpenERP Client*

The client can be installed very easily using the *setup.py* file:

```
tar -xzf openerp-client-6.0.0.tar.gz
cd openerp-client-6.0.0
sudo python setup.py install
```

You can now run the client using the following command:

```
openerp-client
```

*Configuring a PDF Viewer*

To preview PDF files, OpenERP Client by default supports:

1. evince
2. xpdf
3. gpdf
4. kpdf
5. epdfview
6. acroread

The client will try to find one of these executables (in this order) in your system and open the PDF document with it.

**PDF**

For example, if *xpdf*, *kpdf* and *acroread* are the only PDF viewers installed on your system, the OpenERP client will use *xpdf* for previewing PDF documents.

If you want to use another PDF viewer or if you do not want to use the first one the client will find, you have to edit the OpenERP configuration file, normally located in `~/.openerprc`. Find the `[printer]` section and edit the `softpath` parameter. For example:

```
[printer]
softpath = kpdf
```

## 15.4 OpenERP Web Installation

*Downloading the OpenERP Web Client*

The OpenERP Web Client can be downloaded from OpenERP website's download page <http://www.openerp.com/downloads>.

*Installing the required packages*

You need to install the following Python libraries, because OpenERP Web Client uses these packages:

1. Python >= 2.4
2. CherryPy >= 3.1.2
3. Mako >= 0.2.4
4. Babel >= 0.9.4
5. FormEncode >= 1.2.2
6. simplejson >= 2.0.9
7. pyparsing >= 1.5.0

There is no need to install the above packages one by one. You can just run the following commands in your favourite shell:

```
$ sudo apt-get install python python-dev build-essential
$ sudo apt-get install python-setuptools
```

This will install dependencies required for the following:

```
$ cd /path/to/openerp-web-6.0.0/lib
$ ./populate.sh
$ cd ..
```

This will install all required dependencies in private lib directory, and you do not need to install anything.

*Testing the OpenERP Web Client*

If you only want to test the web client, you do not need to install it. Just unpack the archive and start the openerp-web executable:

```
tar -xzf openerp-web-6.0.0.tar.gz
cd openerp-web-6.0.0/
python openerp-web.py
```

The list of available command line parameters can be obtained with the `-h` command line switch:

```
python openerp-web.py -h
```

*Installing the OpenERP Web Client*

The OpenERP Web Client can be installed very easily using the *setup.py* file:

```
tar -xzf openerp-web-6.0.0.tar.gz
cd openerp-web-6.0.0
sudo python setup.py install
```

You can now run the OpenERP Web Client using the following command:

```
openerp-web
```

You can find the OpenERP Web Client configuration file at `~/openerp-web-6.0.0/doc/openerp-web.conf`.

*Web Browser Compatibilities*

## 15.4.1 Supported Browsers

*OpenERP Web Client* is known to work best with *Mozilla* based web browsers. Here is a list of supported browsers:

1. Firefox >= 3.6
2. Internet Explorer >= 7.0
3. Safari >= 4.1
4. Google Chrome >= 9.0
5. Opera >= 10.0

*Flash Plugin*

Your browser should have the Flash plugin installed because *OpenERP Web Client* uses some Flash components.

Apply the following command in order to install the Flash plugin on an Ubuntu system:

```
$ sudo apt-get install flashplugin-nonfree
```

## 15.5 Updating your OpenERP Installation

*Going to a Newer Minor/Patch Release*

OpenERP's release policy states that minor/patch releases of the stable versions are usually published every month. These are recommended for production deployment, as they include the latest security updates and bugfixes, and do not require any migration process.

Of course you should always test these updates on a staging environment (copy of your production environment) before actually applying them on the real production systems.

Minor/patch releases of OpenERP are identified by an increasing 3rd release number, for example, v6.0.15 would be the 15th patch release of OpenERP v6.0.

**Minor Versions**

You can skip minor versions, for example, you do not need to install all the intermediary versions between 6.0.6 and 6.0.15 if you need to upgrade an outdated installation, as long as you stay in the same version line (6.0 in this example).

Updating an existing OpenERP installation to a newer patch release boils down to 2 operations:

- Install the new code over the existing one
- Synchronize each existing database with the new code

In order to accomplish this, the following step-by-step procedure should give you the best results:

1. Make a fresh backup of all existing databases, as well as a backup of the files of your OpenERP installation (server, web and addons), just in case.
2. Locate the executable file to start the Server, it should be named `openerp-server.py`. You may want to have a look at the running processes to find out the command-line parameters that are passed to the server (needed below).
3. Stop the OpenERP server as well as the Web Server (if present).
4. Update the source files to the latest release, or simply install the new releases over the previous ones.
5. Start the server manually (directly call the executable you located above), with the following additional parameters, to trigger an update of all module data and views in the database, based on the new source files (include your usual startup parameters, if any, and replace `DB_NAME` with the name of the OpenERP database you wish to update):

```
openerp-server.py -d DB_NAME -u all
```

6. Let the server complete its startup (watch the log for the final message that says `OpenERP server is running, waiting for connections` or wait until you can connect to that database with a GTK client), then stop the server with `Ctrl+C` and repeat the previous step for each database on this OpenERP installation (any database not updated will use the latest business logic but might have errors or missing improvements in the views until you update it using this procedure).
7. Stop the server again with `Ctrl+C` and restart it normally (no extra parameters anymore).
8. Start the Web Server if present.
9. You can now proceed with the update of the GTK clients, which can be done separately by simply reinstalling the latest version over the previous one.

**Server**

As an alternative to restarting the server in update mode for each database, as described above, you may try to start the server normally, and then connect to each database as the *Administrator* user, open the list of modules and manually trigger an update of the *base* module. Because all modules depend on *base* they will be updated too. However this requires the *Administrator* password of each database and may not work for some updates, specifically when the update prevents you from logging into the system.

**Developer Book**

For more technical details on the actual operations accomplished by the server during such an update, you may refer to the corresponding section in the Developer Book on line.

*Going to a Newer Major Release*

The frequency of major stable releases has fluctuated in the past, but the current policy is to release a new stable version every 6 months on average, with one out of three stable versions being a Long Term Support (LTS) version. An LTS version is a normal stable version, but one that is supported for an extended time under the OpenERP Publisher's Warranty (OPW). Stable versions are labelled as a decimal number with 2 components (e.g. 6.1), where the leftmost part indicates the corresponding Long Term Support (LTS) version, and the second digit indicates successive stable releases between two LTS versions.

Transitioning to the next major release implies a lot more changes than jumping to another minor release. As the underlying OpenERP data structures usually evolve quite a bit from one major release to the next, a full migration of the existing data is needed. Each major release will be published with specific recommendations and procedures for upgrading an existing OpenERP system to the next major version.

# OpenERP Installation on Windows 16

In this chapter, you will see the installation of OpenERP V6.0 on a Windows system. This procedure is well-tested on Windows 7.

You have two options for the installation of OpenERP on a Windows system:

- **All-In-One Installation** This is the easiest way to install OpenERP in the shortest time. It installs all of the components (OpenERP Server, Client, Web and PostgreSQL database) pre-configured on one computer. This installation is recommended if you do not have any major customizations.
- **Independent Installation** If you choose this mode of installation, all the components required to run OpenERP will have to be downloaded and installed separately. You will have to opt for an independent installation if you plan to install the components on separate machines. This mode is also practical if you are already working with or plan to use a different version of PostgreSQL than the one provided with the All-In-One installer.

## 16.1 OpenERP All-In-One Installation

Each time a new release of OpenERP is made, OpenERP supplies a complete Windows auto-installer for it. This contains all of the components you need – the PostgreSQL database server, the OpenERP application server, the GTK application client and the Web client.

This auto-installer enables you to install the whole system in just a few mouse clicks. The initial configuration is set up during installation, making it possible to start using it very quickly, as long as you do not want to change the underlying code. It is aimed at the installation of everything on a single PC, but you can later connect GTK clients from other PCs, Macs and Linux boxes to it as well.

*Downloading OpenERP All-In-One*

The first step is to download the OpenERP All-In-One installer. At this stage, you must choose which version to install – the stable version or the development version. If you are planning to put it straight into production we strongly advise you to choose the stable version.

**Stable Versions and Development Versions**

OpenERP development proceeds in two parallel tracks: stable versions and development versions.

New functionality is integrated into the development branch. This branch is more advanced than the stable branch, but it can contain undiscovered and unfixed faults. A new development release is made every month or so, and OpenERP has made the code repository available so you can download the very latest revisions if you want.

The stable branch is designed for production environments. Here, releases of new functionality are made only about once a year after a long period of testing and validation. Only bug fixes are released through the year on the stable branch.

To download OpenERP for Windows, follow these steps:

1. Navigate to the site http://www.openerp.com.
2. Click the *Downloads* button at the right, then, under *Windows Auto-Installer*, select **All-In-One**.
3. Before you can proceed with the download, you will be asked to fill an online form with your contact and company details and information regarding your interest in OpenERP.
4. Once you submit the online form, the All-In-One Windows installer (currently **openerp-allinone-setup-6.0.2.exe**) becomes available for download.
5. Save the file on your PC - it is quite a substantial size because it downloads everything including the PostgreSQL database system (version 8.3, at the time of writing), so it will take some time.

*Installing the OpenERP All-In-One*

To install OpenERP and its database, you must be signed in as an Administrator on your PC.

If you have previously tried to install the All-In-One version of OpenERP, you will have to uninstall that first, because various elements of a previous installation could interfere with your new installation. Make sure that all Tiny ERP, OpenERP and PostgreSQL applications are removed: you are likely to have to restart your PC to finish removing all traces of them.

Double-click the installer file to install OpenERP and accept the default parameters on each dialog box as you go. The All-In-One installer is the simplest mode of installation and has the following steps:

- 1. **Select installation language** The default is `English`. The other option is `French`.
- 2. **Welcome message** Carefully follow the recommendations given in this step.

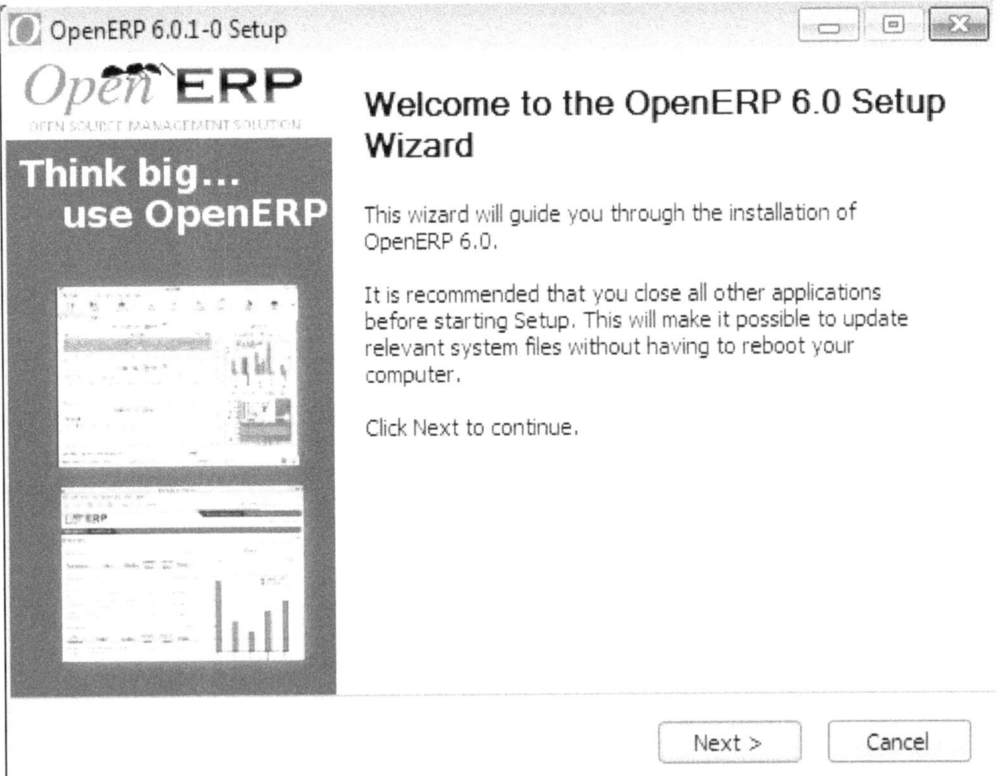


*Welcome to OpenERP*

- 3. **Licence Agreement** It is important that you accept the GNU General Public License to proceed with installation.
- 4. **Select components to install** You can proceed with the default install type `All In One`, which will install the OpenERP Server, GTK Desktop Client, Web Client and PostgreSQL Database (version 8.3, at the time of writing). Or, you may customize your installation by selecting only the components you require.

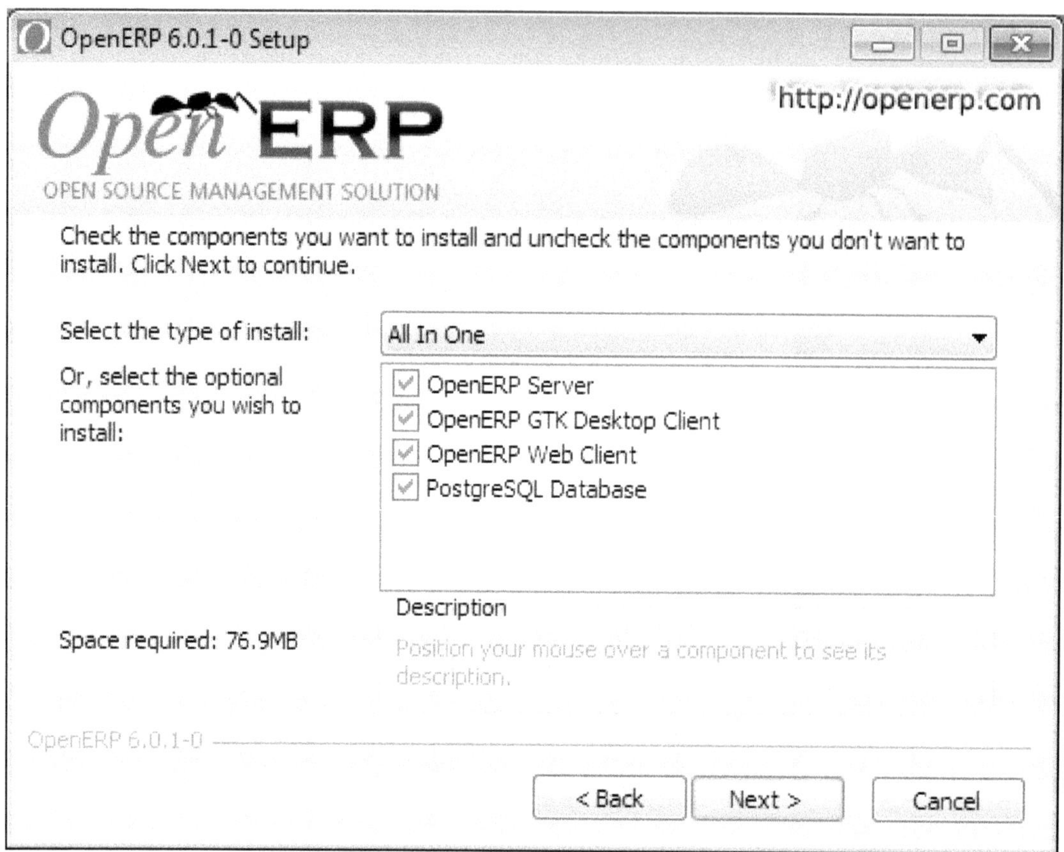


*Customize component installation*

- 5. **Configure PostgreSQL connection** The installer will suggest default parameters to complete your PostgreSQL connection configuration. You may accept the defaults, or change it according to your requirement.

*PostgreSQL configuration*

- 6. **Select folder for installation** By default, OpenERP is installed in `C:\Program Files\OpenERP 6.0`. To install in a different folder, browse for a different location(folder) in this step.
- 7. **Install** The automatic installation of OpenERP begins and you can view its progress simultaneously.
- 8. **Finish** On successful installation of OpenERP, you will get an appropriate confirmation. You can click *Finish* to close the setup wizard.

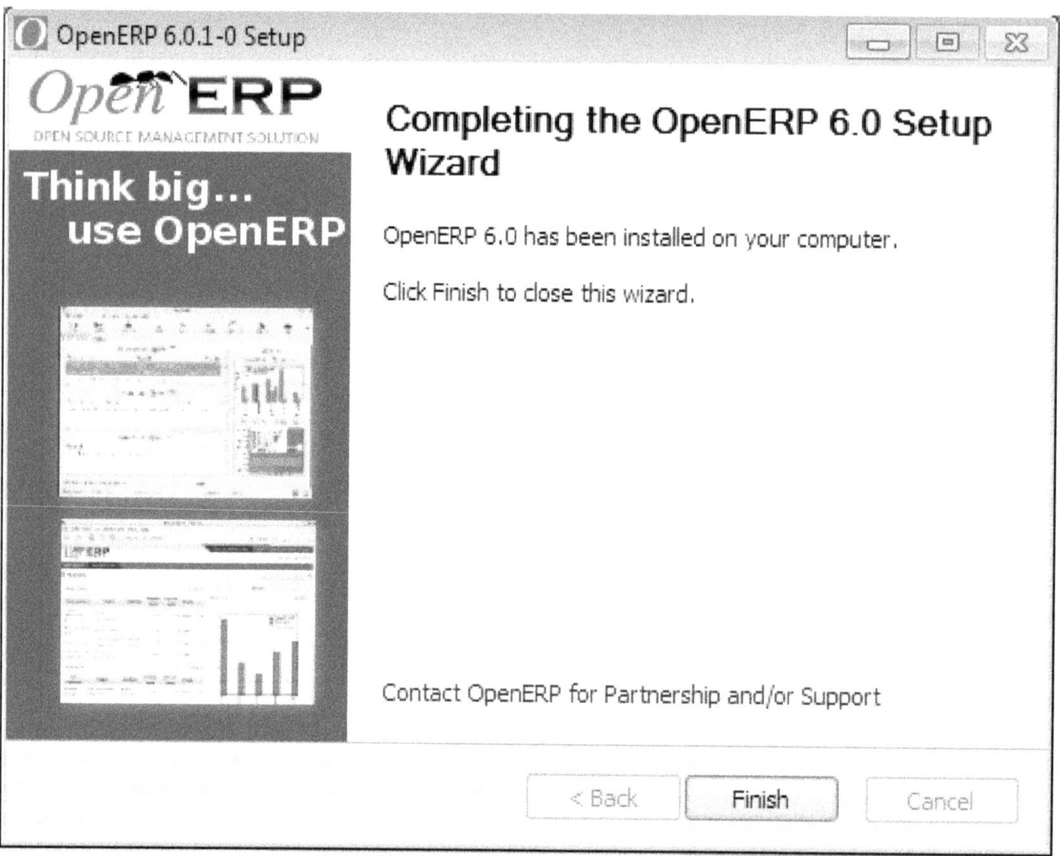


*End of setup wizard*

*Starting the OpenERP Client*

You do not need to manually start the OpenERP Server, because it is installed as a Windows service. But you may trigger various actions from the shortcuts created in the *Start* menu for *OpenERP GTK Client 6.0*, *OpenERP Server 6.0* and *PostgreSQL 8.3*. The OpenERP Client can be opened, ready to use the OpenERP system, once you have completed the All-In-One installation.

You will find the *OpenERP Client* icon on your desktop, which you double-click to access the OpenERP client interface. Use the menu *File* → *Connect...* to connect to a database. As this would be the first time you are using OpenERP since its installation, your database will be empty. You can create a new database through *File* → *Databases* → *New database*.

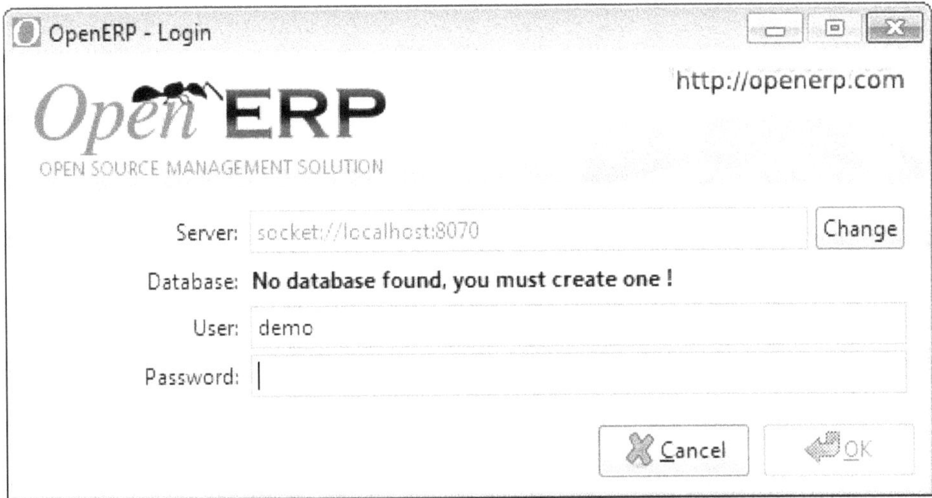


*Database on first run*

## 16.2 PostgreSQL Server Installation and Configuration

In this chapter, you will see how to configure PostgreSQL for its use with OpenERP. The following procedure is well-tested on PostgreSQL v9.0.

*Installing PostgreSQL Server*

You can download the Windows installer from the PostgreSQL download page

Depending on your need, choose either the *One Click Installer* or the *pgInstaller* and run the executable you have just downloaded. *Set up a PostgreSQL User*

When the installations of the required software are done, you have to create a PostgreSQL user. OpenERP will use this user to connect to PostgreSQL.

*Add a User*

Start a Windows console (run the `cmd` command in the *Search programs and files* text box of the *Start* menu).

Change the directory to the *PostgreSQL* `bin` directory (e.g. `C:\Program Files\PostgreSQL\9.0\bin`) or add this directory to your *PATH* environment variable.

The default superuser for PostgreSQL is called *postgres*. His password was chosen during the PostgreSQL installation.

In your Windows console, type:

```
C:\Program Files\PostgreSQL\9.0\bin>createuser.exe --createdb --username postgres --
Enter password for new role: openpgpwd
Enter it again: openpgpwd
Shall the new role be a superuser? (y/n) y
```

```
Password: XXXXXXXXXX
```

```
* line 1 is the command itself
* line 2 asks you the new user's password
* line 3 asks you to confirm the new user's password
* line 4 new role is superuser or not?
* line 5 asks you the *postgres* user's password
```

Option explanations:

- `--createdb` : the new user will be able to create new databases
- `--username postgres` : *createuser* will use the *postgres* user (superuser)
- `--no-createrole` : the new user will not be able to create new users
- `--pwprompt` : *createuser* will ask you the new user's password
- `openpg` : the new user's name. Alternatively, you may specify a different username.
- `openpgpwd` : the new user's password. Alternatively, you may specify a different password.

**Password**

In OpenERP v6, `openpg` and `openpgpwd` are the default username and password used during the OpenERP Server installation. If you plan to change these defaults for the server, or have already installed the server with different values, you have to use those user configuration values when you create a PostgreSQL user for OpenERP.

Now use *pgAdmin III* to create database "openerpdemo" with owner "openpg":

```
CREATE DATABASE openerpdemo WITH OWNER = openpg ENCODING = 'UTF8';
COMMENT ON DATABASE openerpdemo IS 'OpenERP Demo DB';
```

If you have installed the OpenERP Server, you can start it now. If needed, you can override the server configuration by starting the server at a Windows console and specifying command-line options. For more on this, refer the section *sect-custconf*.

To change a user's password in any Windows version, execute the following:

```
net user <accountname> <newpassword>
e.g. net user postgres postgres
```

If it is a domain account, just add "/DOMAIN" at the end.

If you want to delete it, just execute:

```
net user <accountname> /delete
```

*Case-Insensitive Search Issue*

For an installation which needs full UTF8 character support, consider using postgres >= 8.2.x. Using versions prior to this, OpenERP search will eventually not return the expected results for case-insensitive searches, which are used for searching partners, products etc.

Example:

```
SELECT 'x' FROM my_table WHERE 'bét' ilike 'BÉT'
--matches only in 8.2.x
```

## 16.3 OpenERP Server Installation

The OpenERP Server 6.0 installation works with disks formatted in NTFS (not a FAT or FAT32 partition). The following installation procedure has been well-tested on Windows 7.

**Windows Versions**

OpenERP Server does not work on Windows 98 or ME; for obvious reasons – these cannot be formatted using NTFS.

You will need a PostgreSQL server up and running. If it is not the case, you can read the *PostgreSQL Server Installation and Configuration* (page 157) section.

*Downloading the OpenERP Server*

The OpenERP Server can be downloaded from OpenERP website's download page <http://www.openerp.com/downloads>.

Under *Windows Auto-Installer*, choose **Server** to download the OpenERP Server standalone.

*Installing the OpenERP Server*

Execute the installer you have just downloaded. It has the following stages:

- 1. **Select installation language** The default is `English`. The other option is `French`.
- 2. **Welcome message** Carefully follow the recommendations given in this step.
- 3. **Licence Agreement** It is important that you accept the GNU General Public License to proceed with installation.
- 4. **Select folder for installation** By default, OpenERP Server is installed in `C:\Program Files\OpenERP 6.0\Server`. To install in a different folder, browse for a different location(folder) in this step.

- 5. **Configure PostgreSQL connection** The installer will suggest default parameters to complete your PostgreSQL connection configuration. You may accept the defaults, or change it according to your requirement.

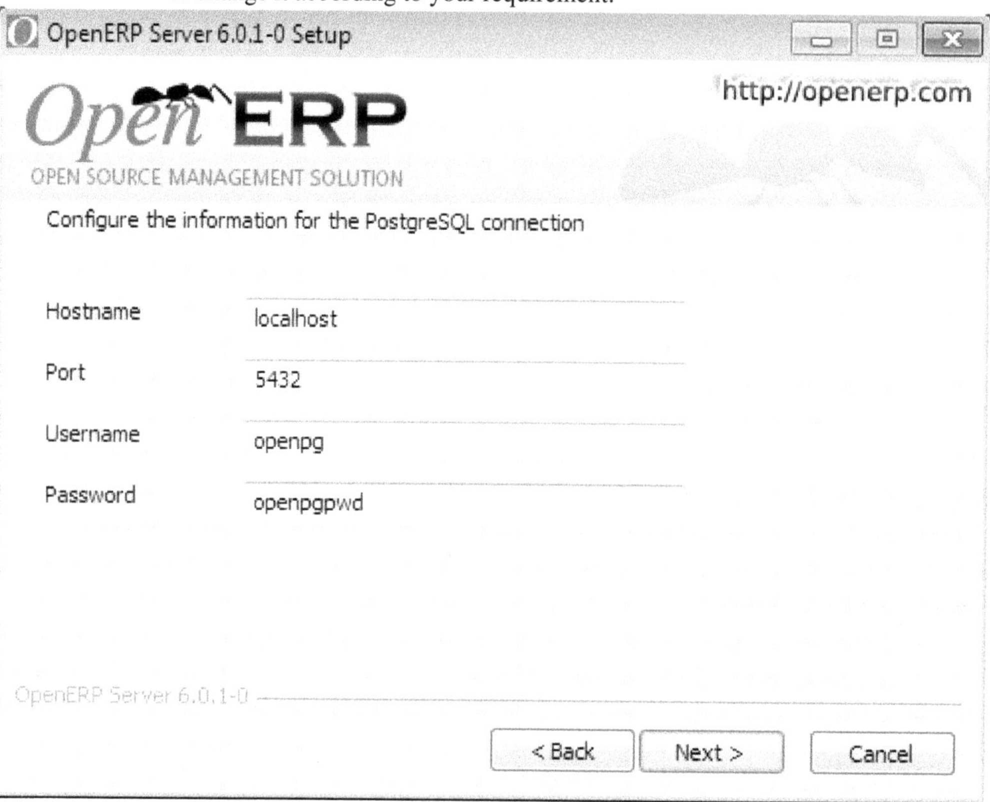


*PostgreSQL configuration*

- 6. **Create shortcuts** Select a folder in the *Start* menu where you would like to create the program's shortcuts.

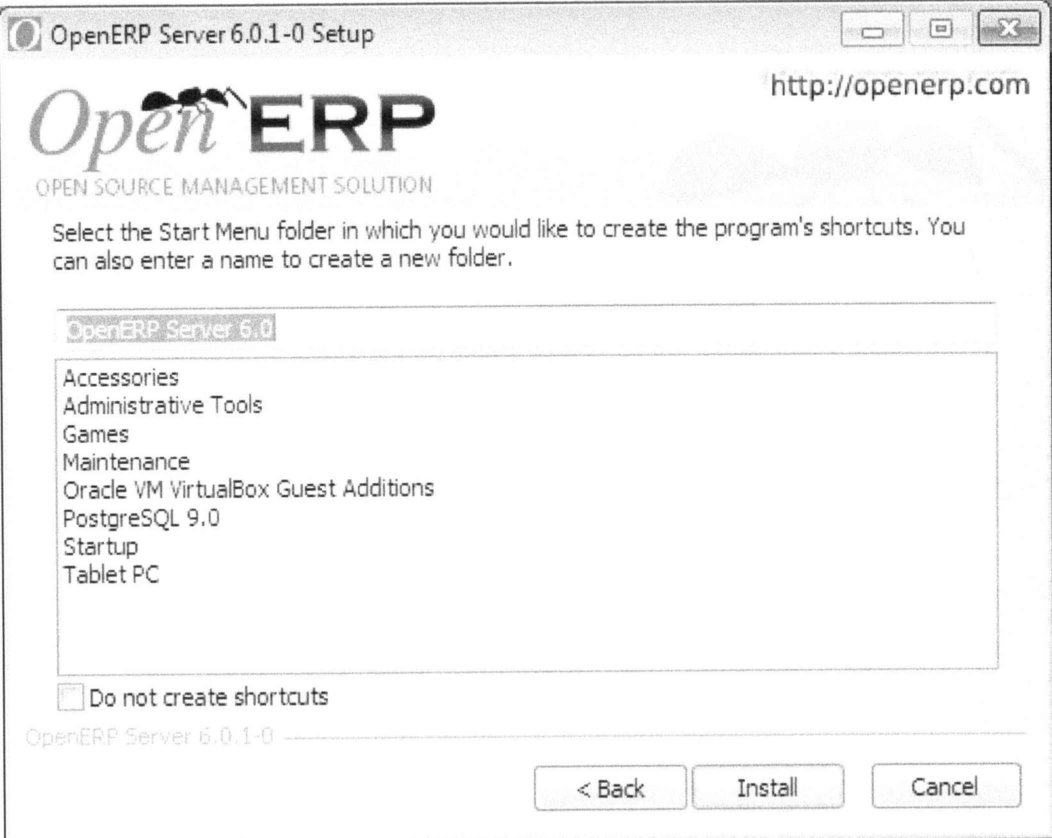


*Create Start menu shortcuts*

- 7. **Install** The automatic installation of OpenERP Server begins and you can view its progress simultaneously.
- 8. **Finish** On successful installation of OpenERP Server, you will get an appropriate confirmation. You can click *Finish* to close the setup wizard.

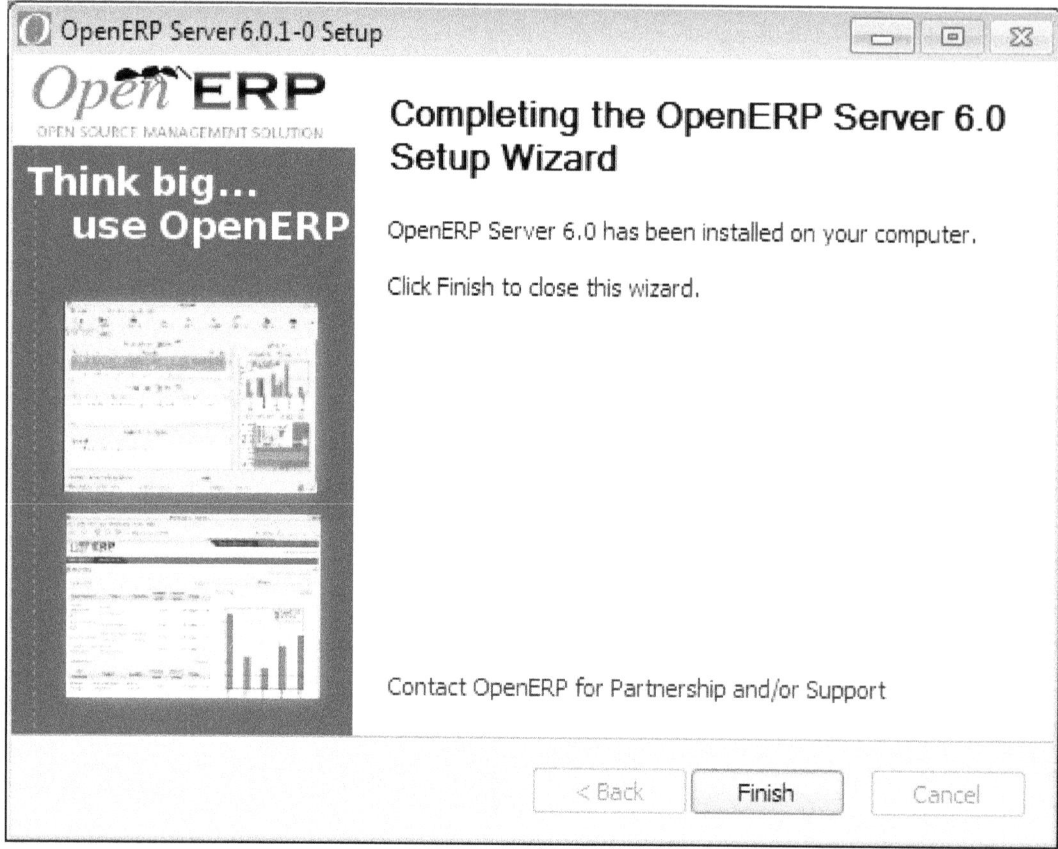


*End of setup wizard*

The OpenERP Server also installs as a Windows service. This means you do not have to start the server each time you start the computer and it runs without the need of an open user session. *Customized Configuration*

To initialize the server with configurations of your choice, you have to invoke it at the Windows Command prompt with the options you wish to override.

Navigate to the installation directory in `C:\Program Files\OpenERP 6.0\Server\` and type this command but do not execute it yet:

```
openerp-server.exe -d <db_name> -r <db_user> -w <db_password>
--db_host=<postgresql_server_address>
--db_port=<port_no> --logfile="<logfile>"
```

The initialization of OpenERP Server provides necessary information for connection to the PostgreSQL database and the choice of data to load. Here is the explanation of used options:

- `-d <db_name>` : Name of the database created for OpenERP Server.
- `-r <db_user>` : Name of the PostgreSQL user (role).

- -w <db_password> : Password of the PostgreSQL user.
- --db_host=<postgresql_server_address> : Address of the server where PostgreSQL is. If you have installed PostgreSQL on the same computer as OpenERP Server, you can enter localhost, else, the IP address or the name of the distant server.
- --db_port=<port_no> : Port number where PostgreSQL listens. The default is 5432.
- --stop-after-init : This option stops the server after initialization.
- --logfile="<logfile>" : specify an alternate logfile where all the output of server will be saved. The default is C:\Program Files\OpenERP 6.0\Server\openerp-server.log.

Before the execution of this command you have to decide the purpose of the database created in OpenERP.

Sample command:

```
openerp-server.exe -d openerpdemo -r openpg -w openpgpwd
--db_host=localhost --logfile="C:\Users\tiny\Desktop\demo_db.log"
--db_port=5430 --stop-after-init
```

Here you have to enter the username and password specified in the PostgreSQL connection configuration during server installation.

When you execute the initialization command, if you specify a logfile, the server runtime output is written to that file, and you will not see any server output in the prompt window. You have only to wait until the prompt comes back.

*Deciding about the Purpose of the Database*

You can initialize the database with OpenERP Server to:

1. Take a look at the system with modules installed and demo data loaded
2. Install a new clean database system (without demo data)
3. Upgrade an existing version

*With modules and demo data*

If you execute the sample command above, you will get a database with only base modules installed and loaded with demo data. To initialize OpenERP Server with additional modules and its demo data, you need to add this option to the above command:

```
-i <module name>
```

Sample command:

```
openerp-server.exe -d openerpdemo --stop-after-init -i sale
```

This command will initialize the OpenERP Server with the module `sale` and its dependencies, and fill its PostgreSQL database with their related demo data. As can be seen, you must specify the target database for the module installation.

To install more than one module, specify a comma-separated module list at the command-line.

*Without demo data (or new clean version)*

Execute the command with an option excluding the demo data:

```
--without-demo=all
```

This will load base modules (and other modules if -i option is used), but will not load its demo data.

Sample command usage:

```
openerp-server.exe -d openerpdemo --stop-after-init --without-demo=all
```

If you have already initialized the database with demo data loaded, you can create a new database and execute the above command on it.

*Update the database*

Execute the command with an option that updates the data structures:

```
--update=all
```

Sample command usage:

```
openerp-server.exe -d openerpdemo --stop-after-init --update=all
```

*Monitoring the OpenERP Server*

The service and some runtime information is accessible through the Computer Management console in Administrative Tools.

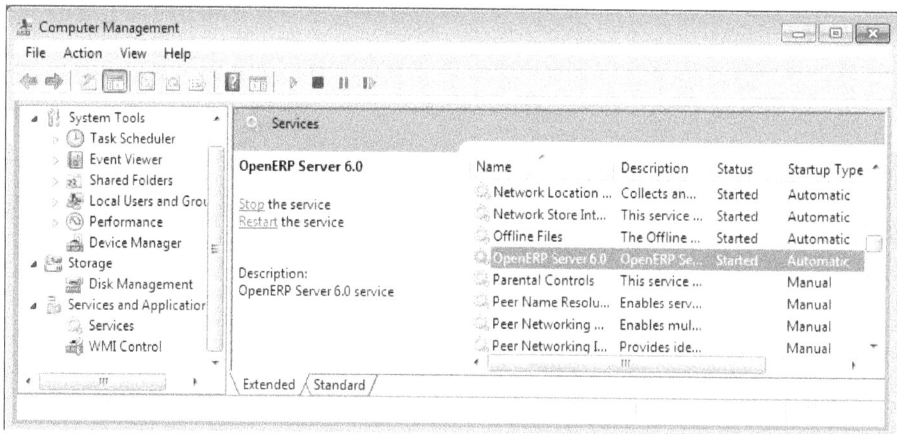


*OpenERP Server 6.0 in the Services list*

Here, you can define how the service should act in case of server failure. Access the service's properties by double-clicking `OpenERP Server 6.0` in the list.

*Recovery tab to set service failure response*

The Computer Management logging service offers additional information about the execution of the OpenERP Server, for example, the startup or shutdown information of the service.

*Server information in Windows Logs list*

OpenERP Server runtime output can be found in the default logfile. Given that the server is now

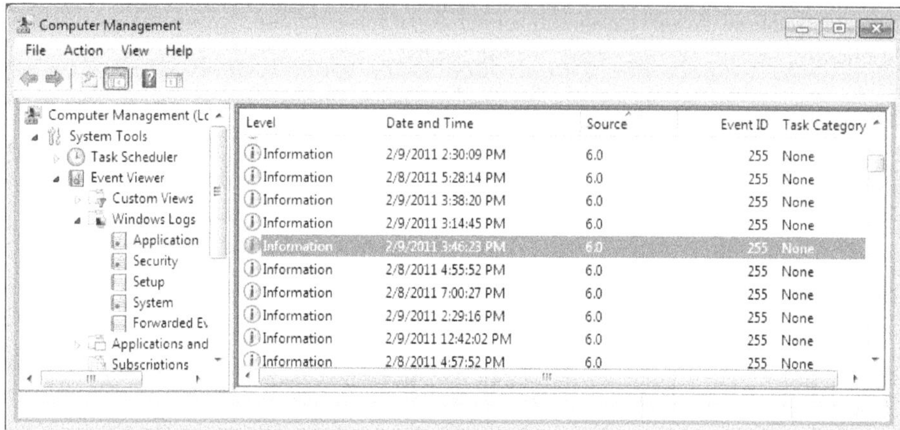


running as a Windows service, it does not output any runtime messages. For this, the logfile is the only option. Access it from the *Start* menu, through the `View log` link in the group of shortcuts for OpenERP Server 6.0. Alternatively, use the path `C:\Program Files\OpenERP 6.0\Server\openerp-server.log`.

```
openerp-server - Notepad
File Edit Format View Help
[2011-02-10 14:14:40,013][?] INFO:server:OpenERP version - 6.0.1
[2011-02-10 14:14:40,013][?] INFO:server:addons_path - C:\Program
Files\OpenERP 6.0\Server\addons
[2011-02-10 14:14:40,013][?] INFO:server:database hostname - localhost
[2011-02-10 14:14:40,013][?] INFO:server:database port - 5432
[2011-02-10 14:14:40,013][?] INFO:server:database user - openpg
[2011-02-10 14:14:40,013][?] INFO:server:initialising distributed
objects services
[2011-02-10 14:14:45,200][?] INFO:server:OpenERP version - 6.0.1
[2011-02-10 14:14:45,210][?] INFO:server:addons_path - C:\Program
Files\OpenERP 6.0\Server\addons
[2011-02-10 14:14:45,210][?] INFO:server:database hostname - localhost
[2011-02-10 14:14:45,210][?] INFO:server:database port - 5432
[2011-02-10 14:14:45,210][?] INFO:server:database user - openpg
[2011-02-10 14:14:45,210][?] INFO:server:initialising distributed
objects services
[2011-02-10 14:14:46,361][?] INFO:web-services:starting HTTP service at
0.0.0.0 port 8069
[2011-02-10 14:14:46,371][?] INFO:web-services:starting HTTPS service
at 0.0.0.0 port 8071
[2011-02-10 14:14:46,371][?] INFO:web-services:Registered XML-RPC over
HTTP
[2011-02-10 14:14:46,371][?] INFO:web-services:starting NET-RPC service
at 0.0.0.0 port 8070
[2011-02-10 14:14:46,371][?] INFO:server:Starting 3 services
[2011-02-10 14:14:46,381][?] INFO:server:OpenERP server is running,
waiting for connections...
```

*OpenERP Server log file*

You can find out whether OpenERP Server is running by invoking *Windows Task Manager*. When you look at the *Processes* tab, you will see `OpenERPServerService.exe` and `openerp-server.exe`, both having `SYSTEM` as their user (to see these, *Show processes from all users* must be enabled in the Task Manager).

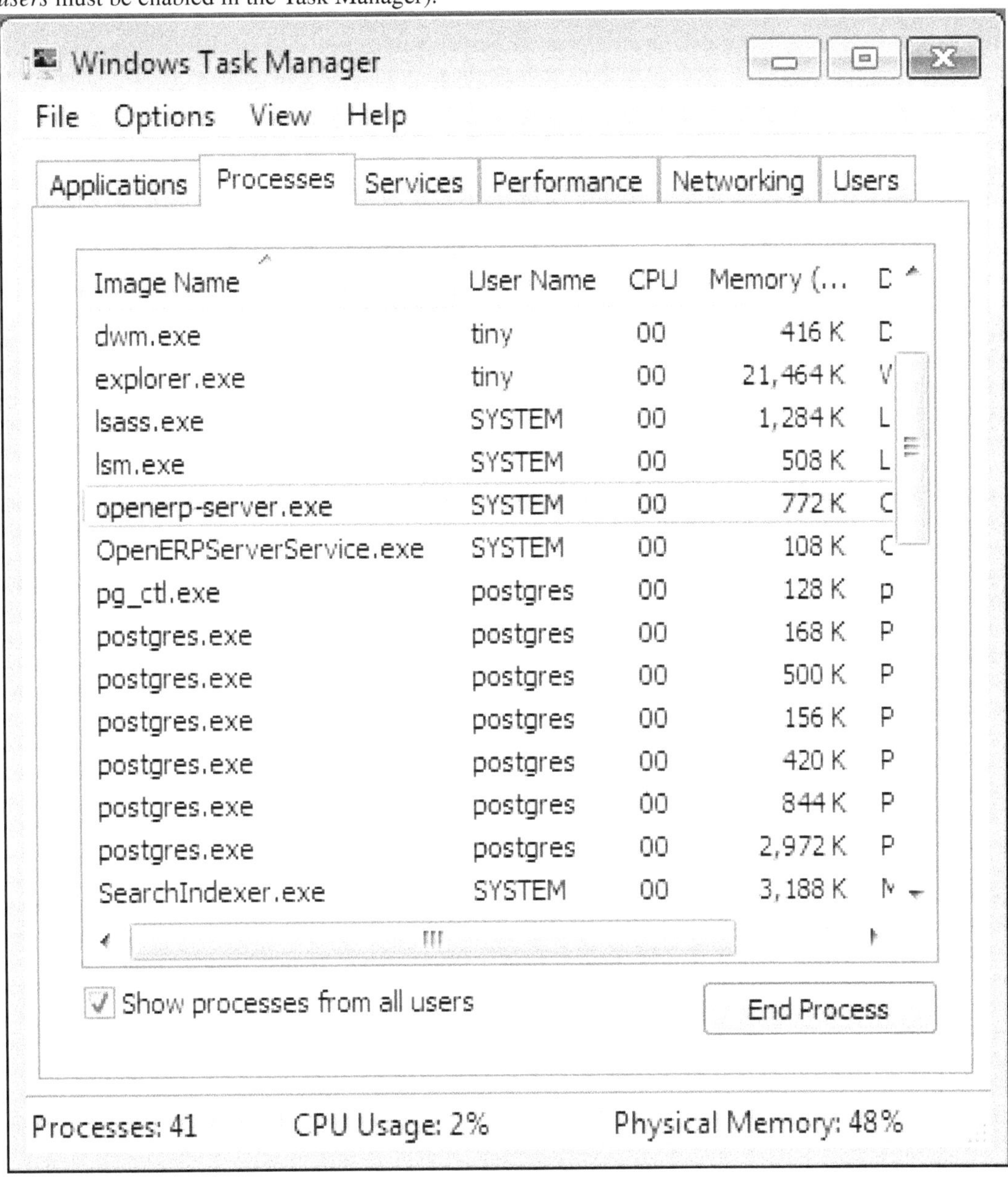


*The services in Windows Task Manager*

**Congratulations, you have successfully installed OpenERP Server**

For more information, please take a look at *Additional Installation Information and Troubleshooting* (page 174), where you can find some troubleshooting examples.

## 16.4 OpenERP Client Installation

You have to install, configure and run the OpenERP Server before using the OpenERP Client. The client needs the server to run. You can install the server application on your computer, or on an independent server accessible by network.

*Downloading the OpenERP Client*

The OpenERP Client can be downloaded from OpenERP website's download page.

Under *Windows Auto-Installer*, choose **Client** to download the OpenERP Client standalone.

*Installing the OpenERP Client*

Click the executable installation file you have just downloaded, and proceed with the following steps:

- 1. **Select installation language** The default is `English`. The other option is `French`.
- 2. **Welcome message** Carefully follow the recommendations given in this step.
- 3. **Licence Agreement** It is important that you accept the GNU General Public License to proceed with installation.
- 4. **Select folder for installation** By default, OpenERP Client is installed in `C:\Program Files\OpenERP 6.0\Client`. To install in a different folder, browse for a different location(folder) in this step.
- 5. **Create shortcuts** Select a folder in the *Start* menu where you would like to create the program's shortcuts.

*Create Start menu shortcuts*

- 6. **Install** The automatic installation of OpenERP Client begins and you can view its progress simultaneously.
- 7. **Finish** On successful installation of OpenERP Client, you will get an appropriate confirmation. You can click *Finish* to close the setup wizard.

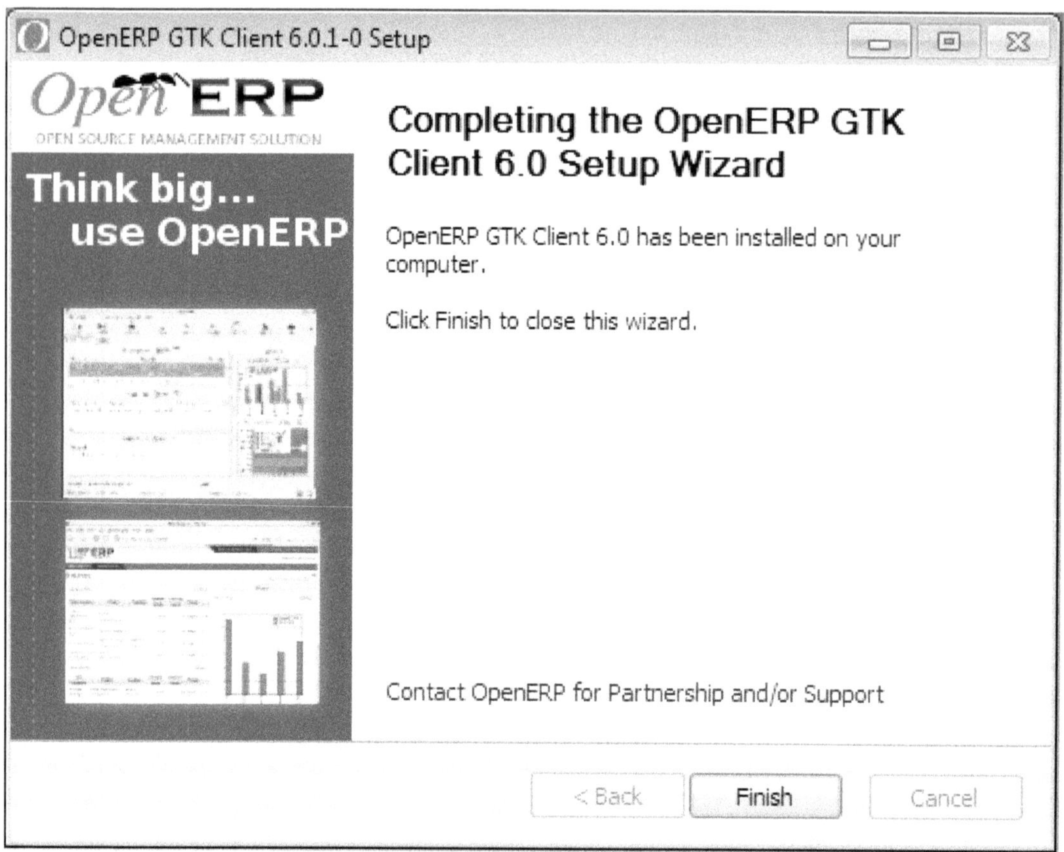


*End of setup wizard*

*Starting the OpenERP Client*

The installation program creates shortcuts in the main program menu and on the desktop, which you can use to start the client. Be sure to have an OpenERP Server running somewhere (on your computer or on a distant server) to be able to use the client software.

Log in to `openerpdemo` database using default username and password:

- Username = admin
- Password = admin

Enjoy!

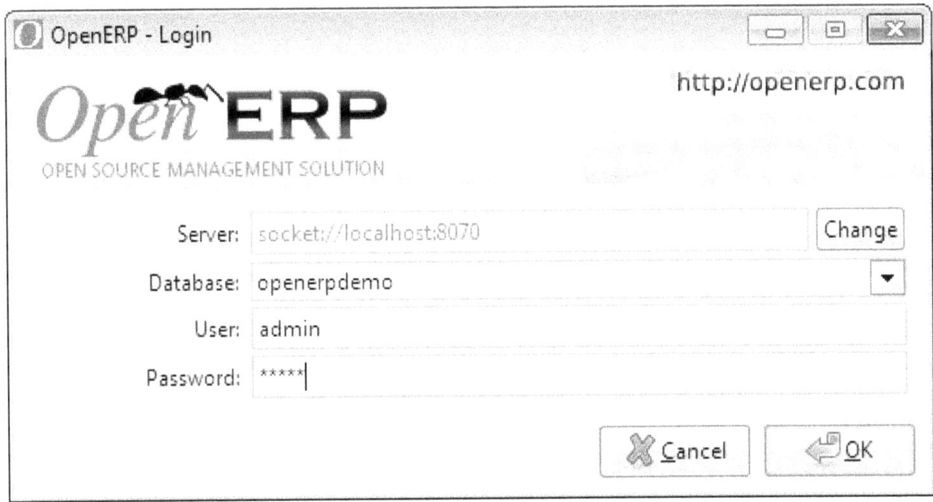


*Connecting to the demo database*

## 16.5 OpenERP Web Installation

You have to install, configure and run the OpenERP Server before using the OpenERP Web. The web client needs the server to run. You can install the server application on your computer, or on an independent server accessible by network.

*Downloading the OpenERP Web*

The OpenERP Web can be downloaded from OpenERP website's download page.

Under *Windows Auto-Installer*, choose **Web** to download the OpenERP Web standalone.

*Installing the OpenERP Web*

Click the executable installation file you have just downloaded, and proceed with the following steps:

- 1. **Select installation language** The default is `English`. The other option is `French`.
- 2. **Welcome message** Carefully follow the recommendations given in this step.
- 3. **Licence Agreement** It is important that you accept the OpenERP Public License (OEPL) Version 1.1 to proceed with installation. This licence is based on the Mozilla Public Licence (MPL) Version 1.1.

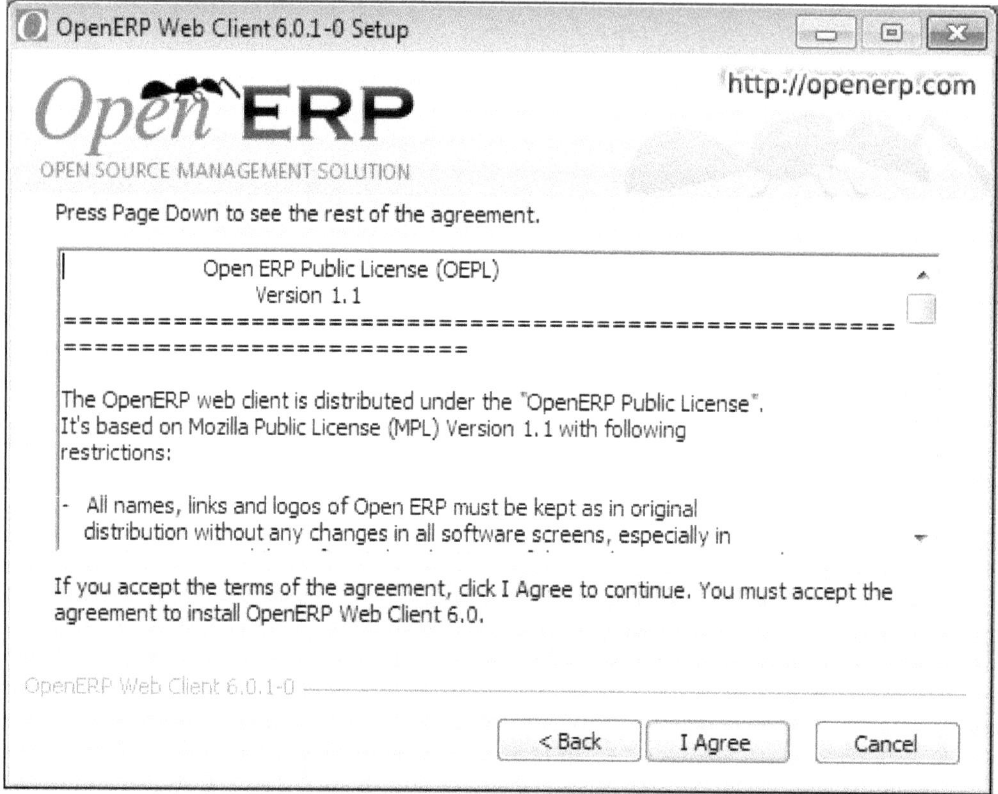


*OpenERP Public Licence*

- 4. **Select folder for installation** By default, OpenERP Web is installed in `C:\Program Files\OpenERP 6.0\Web`. To install in a different folder, browse for a different location(folder) in this step.
- 5. **Create shortcuts** Select a folder in the *Start* menu where you would like to create the program's shortcuts.

*Create Start menu shortcuts*

- 6. **Install** The automatic installation of OpenERP Web begins and you can view its progress simultaneously.
- 7. **Finish** On successful installation of OpenERP Web, you will get an appropriate confirmation. You can click *Finish* to close the setup wizard.

The Windows service for OpenERP Web Server is also installed and is set up to start the server automatically on system boot.

*Starting the Web Client*

Now as the web server is initialized and the settings are saved, you can finally start the OpenERP Web.

Use a web browser of your choice to connect to OpenERP Web. If your web client is installed on the same computer as the server, you can navigate to http://localhost:8080 to connect to the OpenERP web version. If the server is installed on a separate computer, you must know the name or IP address of the server over the network and navigate to http://<server_address>:8080 to connect to OpenERP.

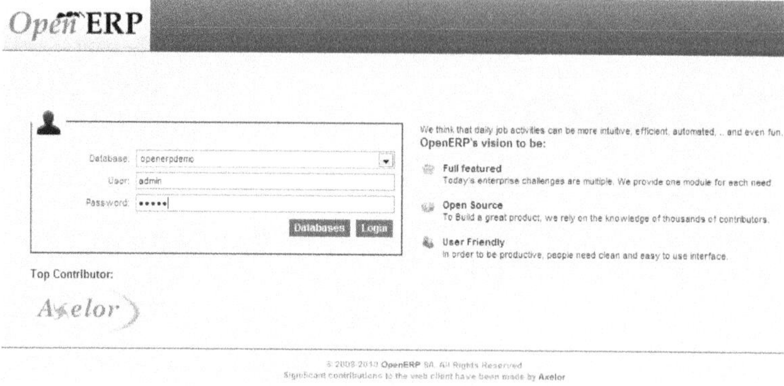


Figure 16.1: *Web Client at startup*

## 16.6 Troubleshooting and Windows Complementary Install Information

*PostgreSQL Administration*

OpenERP Server Connection Error with PostgreSQL

If you are initializing a database from the command-line with a custom username/role (-r) and password (-w), ensure that you have created a corresponding PostgreSQL user for the same. Else, you may encounter error messages as shown below:

```
C:\Windows\system32\cmd.exe

C:\Program Files\OpenERP 6.0\Server>openerp-server.exe -d openerpdemo -r NewUser
 -w NewPass --stop-after-init
Traceback (most recent call last):
  File "openerp-server.py", line 121, in <module>
  File "pooler.pyo", line 39, in get_db_and_pool
  File "addons\__init__.pyo", line 803, in load_modules
  File "sql_db.pyo", line 345, in cursor
  File "sql_db.pyo", line 95, in __init__
  File "sql_db.pyo", line 252, in _locked
  File "sql_db.pyo", line 303, in borrow
psycopg2.OperationalError: FATAL:  password authentication failed for user "NewU
ser"

C:\Program Files\OpenERP 6.0\Server>
```

*User authentication failure*

You may also face another problem similar to this situation:

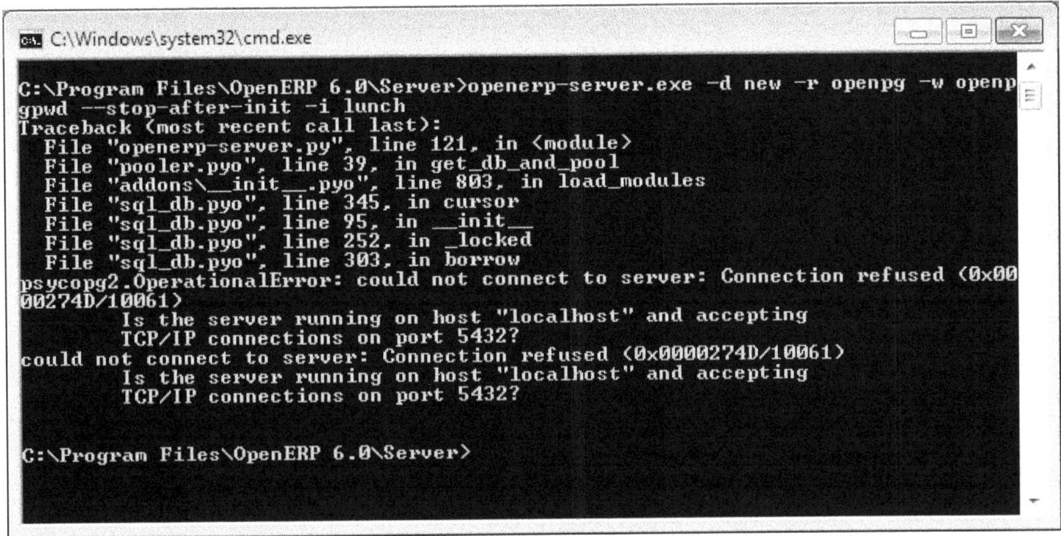


*Database connection failure*

In this case, you should have a look if the service `postgresql-9.0 - PostgreSQL Server 9.0` is running in the Services Manager (*Control Panel → System and Security → Administrative Tools → Services*).

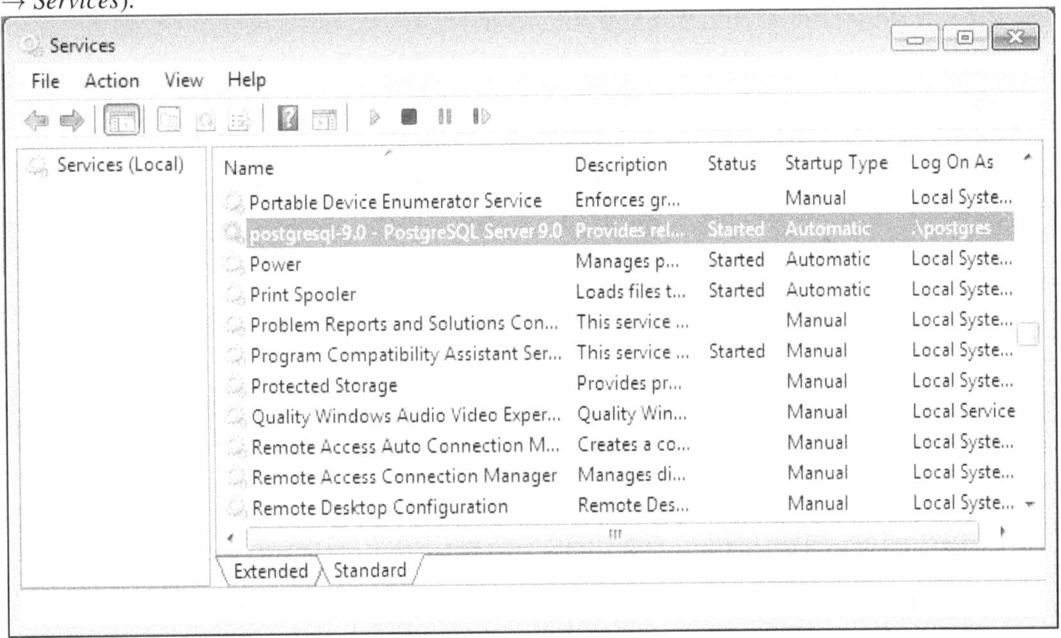


*PostgreSQL 9.0 in the Services list*

You can edit the service configuration to have PostgreSQL start as a service at system boot. This is usually a default.

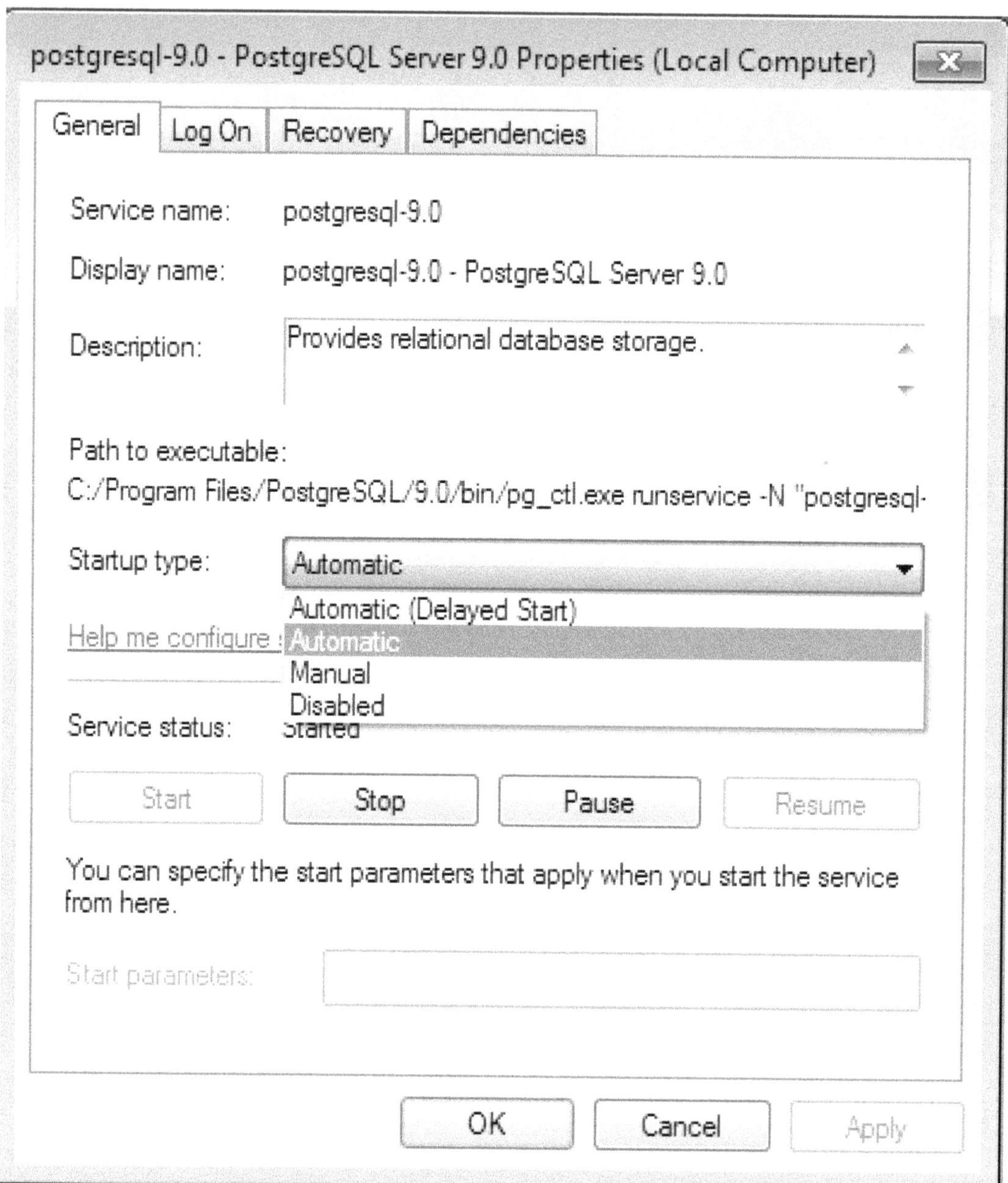


*Configure PostgreSQL 9.0 service*

If your PostgreSQL service is running, but you get connection errors, you can restart the service.

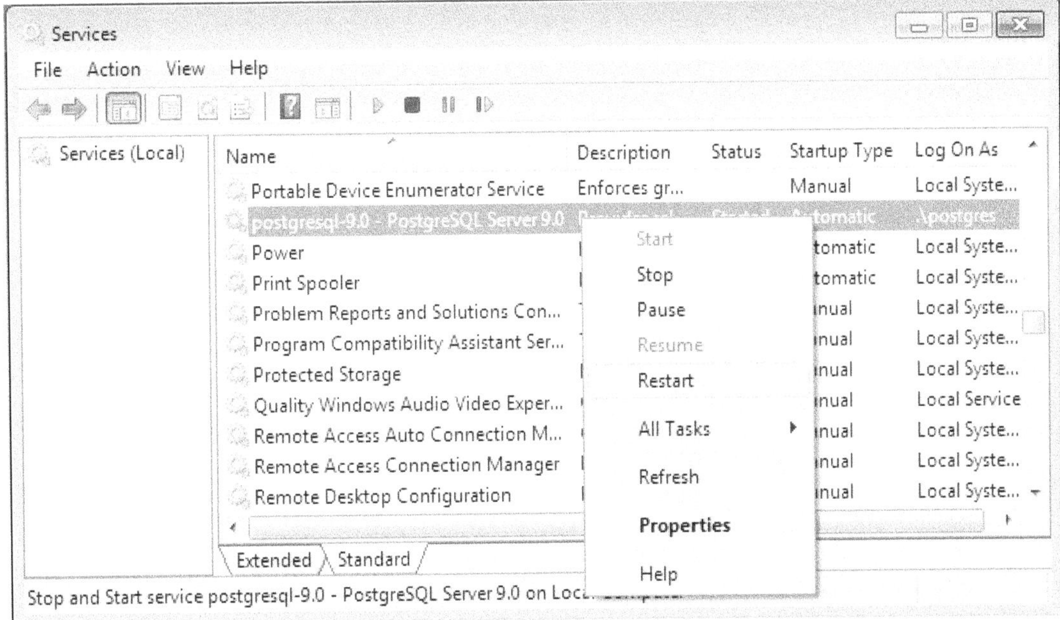


*Restarting the service*

## 16.7 Updating your OpenERP Installation

*Going to a Newer Minor/Patch Release*

OpenERP's release policy states that minor/patch releases of the stable versions are usually published every month. These are recommended for production deployment, as they include the latest security updates and bugfixes, and do not require any migration process.

Of course you should always test these updates on a staging environment (copy of your production environment) before actually applying them on the real production systems.

For more details regarding the release cycle, have a look at the section *release_cycle*.

Minor/patch releases of OpenERP are identified by an increasing 3rd release number, for example, v6.0.15 would be the 15th patch release of OpenERP v6.0.

**Minor Versions**

**You can skip minor versions, for example, you do not need to install** all the intermediary versions between 6.0.6 and 6.0.15 if you need to upgrade an outdated installation, as long as you stay in the same version line (6.0 in this example).

Updating an existing OpenERP installation to a newer patch release boils down to 2 operations:

- Install the new code over the existing one
- Synchronize each existing database with the new code

In order to accomplish this, the following step-by-step procedure should give you the best results:

1. Make a fresh backup of all existing databases, as well as a backup of the files of your OpenERP installation (server, web and addons), just in case.
2. Stop the OpenERP server as well as Web Server (if present).
3. Update the source files to the latest release, or simply install the new releases over the previous ones. If need be, you can uninstall the previous version, but be sure to avoid uninstalling PostgreSQL, as this could result in the deletion of your current databases!
4. Locate the separate server executable `openerp-server.exe` (this is not the executable used by the Windows Service!). It should be in the location where you installed OpenERP Server, for example in `C:\Programs\OpenERP 6.0\Server`.
5. From a Command-Line Prompt, start the server executable manually (directly call the executable you located above), with the following parameters, to trigger an update of all module data and views in the database, based on the new source files (include your usual startup parameters, if any, and replace `DB_NAME` with the name of the OpenERP database you wish to update):

   ```
   openerp-server.exe -d DB_NAME -u all
   ```

6. Let the server complete its startup (watch the log file for the final message that says `OpenERP server is running, waiting for connections` or wait until you can connect to that database with a GTK client), then stop the server using the `Ctrl+C` key combination and repeat previous step for each database on this OpenERP installation (any database not updated will use the latest business logic but might have errors or missing improvements in the views until you update it using this procedure).
7. Stop the server again with `Ctrl+C` and restart it normally as a service.
8. Start the Web Server if present.
9. You can now proceed with the update of the GTK clients, which can be done separately by simply reinstalling the latest version over the previous one.

**Server**

**As an alternative to restarting the server in update mode for each database,** as described above, you may try to start the server normally after installing the new version, and then connect to each database as the *Administrator* user, open the list of modules and manually trigger an update of the *base* module. Because all modules depend on *base* they will be updated too. However this requires the *Administrator* password of each database and may not work for some updates, specifically when the update prevents you from logging into the system.

**Developer Book**

**For more technical details on the actual operations accomplished by the server** during such an update, you may refer to the corresponding section in the Developer Book on line.

*Going to a Newer Major Release*

OpenERP's release policy states that one or two major releases are published from the development version every year. Transitioning to the next major release implies a lot more changes than jumping to another minor release. As the underlying OpenERP data structures usually evolve quite a bit from one major release to the next, a full migration of the existing data is needed. Each major release will be published with specific recommendations and procedures for upgrading an existing OpenERP system to the next major version.

**Major Release**

**For major releases, it is usually not possible to skip one release, for example** upgrading directly from OpenERP 4.2 to OpenERP 6.0. If you need to do such an upgrade, you will simply have to do each intermediary upgrade one after the other.

# Conclusion

Until now only two main alternatives existed for systems managing all of a company's information: install a proprietary ERP system, complete but usually overweight, inflexible, and expensive; or develop a solution internally, adapted to current needs but often expensive to develop and to maintain, not integrated, and incomplete.

With its free business model, OpenERP combines the advantages of a complete ERP system with the flexibility of an in-house solution. The open source code, the project's general flexibility, and its hundreds of modules let you construct a solution from a selection of Business Applications, integrating the modules already available. To sustain your growth, you can freely update your OpenERP application to fit your ever changing needs.

The results will be at the top end of what you might expect from any ERP system, let alone an Open Source system. The considerable gains in productivity, efficiency and visibility become apparent only a few months after implementation. And you can gain from increased operational quality. Because there are fewer repetitive tasks for your staff to do, they can concentrate on higher added-value work. We frequently receive the gratitude of senior management who get better results from their business because they have adopted OpenERP.

Proprietary software vendors drive on average 25% of their revenues from Licenses. Instead, OpenERP revenues are services-based.

Our Open Source model allows us to maintain a lower cost structure thanks to:

- An Efficient Development Model: we leverage from the improvements in the software driven by our customers and community members. As a result more than 700 modules have been developed to date. The software is available in 22 languages and more than 1000 individuals contribute to OpenERP,
- A Volume-based Sales Model: the software can be downloaded for free. Thousands of customers from over 50 countries test it every month and when the time is right for them, they choose to implement our solution. This allows us to reduce very significantly our sales and marketing costs compared to other vendors,
- A single platform for both on line and on site: OpenERP has been designed from the start to be used either on line or on site. This is not the case for most vendors, who need to carry their legacy software and cannot leverage from the web.

The absence of license revenues is more than offset by the benefits driven from the Open Source model.

## You are not alone

Many resources are at hand to accompany you on your OpenERP adventure. The software can be downloaded for free, but we will never claim that deploying an ERP can be done for free. It requires services from OpenERP and its partners.

## The available resources

Larger companies often prefer a more classic implementation path. Even though OpenERP's ease-of-use makes this task easier than with other systems, you cannot hide the fact that a project implementation is complex and introduces big changes to a company.

So you can turn towards some of the different actors in this free software ecosystem to help you out:

- the community of users and developers,
- OpenERP's partners,
- the main project developers, OpenERP, themselves.

### The Community of Users and Developers

The community, supported by OpenERP, hosts a set of communication tools which can help you to discover the OpenERP software.

- **The forum**: http://www.openerp.com/forum/

The forum enables you to discuss issues with other OpenERP users. It is very active and your contributions are very welcome.

- **Online Documentation**: http://doc.openerp.com

This documentation includes various topics: how to use OpenERP, how to develop on OpenERP, how to install OpenERP and much more.

- **OpenERP Apps**: http://apps.openerp.com/

A list of available modules and their descriptions.

- **Launchpad** : https://code.launchpad.net/~openobject/

The most recent communication tool is the launchpad system, which now hosts all of OpenERP's source code (using the *bzr* source code control system) and is used for reporting bugs. It has become the central location for OpenERP technology.

### OpenERP Partners

If you need contractual guarantees for implementing and maintaining OpenERP, you can contact an official OpenERP partner. OpenERP partners offer various services such as user training, prototype installations, and change management services. The complete list of partners by country and by type can be found on the official OpenERP site: http://www.openerp.com/partners.

## The Main Developer, OpenERP

Finally you can call the main project developers, OpenERP, who can help you in your OpenERP project. OpenERP offers various services such as free demonstration days for the software, user training and technical training, support contracts, maintenance contracts. Depending on the demand, OpenERP can also put you in contact with partners most in line with your requirements.

Do not forget that OpenERP has more than seven hundred modules available and that only some business applications are covered in this book. So if you have not found a answer to your questions here, please check http://apps.openerp.com/, talk to other OpenERP users on the forum, and certainly do not hesitate to contact a partner.

Wishing you the greatest of success in your ERP project,

— Els Van Vossel and Fabien Pinckaers.

# Index

www.ingramcontent.com/pod-product-compliance
Ingram Content Group UK Ltd.
Pitfield, Milton Keynes, MK11 3LW, UK
UKHW050920270726
13994UKWH00011B/2452